Finding
the Light
in Deep Waters
and Dark Times

Finding the Light

in Deep Waters and Dark Times

Favorite Talks from
Especially for Youth

BOOKCRAFT
Salt Lake City, Utah

Appreciation is expressed to each of the contributors to this work. In addition to sharing their thoughts and testimonies with youth through the written word, these authors also spend many hours speaking to and directing activities for young people throughout the United States.

Neither The Church of Jesus Christ of Latter-day Saints, the Church Educational System, nor Brigham Young University endorses this work in any way. Each of the contributing authors accepts complete personal responsibility for the contents of his or her chapter.

Library of Congress Catalog Card Number: 92-71302
ISBN 0-88494-839-0

First Printing, 1992

Printed in the United States of America

Contents

CHAPTER 1

That's What Friends Are For

Vickey Pahnke

Who are your friends? And how do you know? Do they bring out the best in you? Are they there for you when you need them? Have you ever been burned by someone you thought you could trust? What are friends for, anyway?

Life can be a lot easier when we have friends to share with us, cry with us, laugh with us, and reassure us that we are okay . . . even when we make mistakes.

My daughter once said to me: "Mom, I'm so embarrassed I could just die. I'll never be able to hang around with my friends again." I told her: "Honey, embarrassing moments run in our family. Your friends know to expect such things from you. And, Andrea, if a person could die from embarrassment, I would have been dead a long time ago."

You need to understand that my life has been a series of humiliating incidents. When I first came to Utah as a student I decided I would leave the "old" me at home in Virginia and start anew. This was flawed thinking—I failed to realize that I was bringing myself with me. Let me illustrate.

At my first ward meeting at BYU I saw this awesome guy, a really good-looking returned missionary. He seemed to have credibility because he was the ward clerk. What could I do to catch his eye? Was I in luck! As a member of the Relief Society presidency, I had been asked to speak in church the next Sunday. Here was my chance to prepare diligently, deliver sweetly, and impress this young man with my spirituality! (Yes, I know my reasoning left something to be desired.) On Sunday, as I stood at the podium, I looked down on the front row to see "my" young man grinning up at me. As I shared my remarks we exchanged smiles. I thought, "Yes! This is working! He wants to know who I am!"

I concluded, and as I began confidently down the steps that would take me directly past him, the heel broke on my shoe. I slid down the steps, sprawling at the feet of the young ward clerk. Agghh! The truth was out! Now the entire ward knew the real me—I was as klutzy in Utah as I had been in Virginia. I was *so* embarrassed. It didn't take long for everyone to learn that if they wanted to have fun they should hang around me . . . *something* would happen that would make them laugh.

Just the next week we decided to go roller skating. What a blast! I had never done this before! At that time I had very long hair, which can be a pain to wash and style every day. For the outing I decided to put a zillion pins in my hair to hold it up, and wear a wig.

As the others skated with great abandon I clung to the railing for dear life. But gradually, with confidence growing, I let go and picked up a little speed. This was fun! This was awesome! I could do it! I didn't realize that at one spot in the rink the flooring didn't quite fit together. As I skated along, increasing in pace and confidence, I hit this uneven flooring. My feet flew up, I landed on my backside, and the wig flew off my head.

The whole place came to a standstill. Everyone simultaneously stifled a laugh/gasp. The fellow who skates around to keep order came to me, picked up my wig, and asked, "Does this belong to you?" I was so embarrassed I thought I would die. But I didn't . . . I merely provided another good laugh for my new friends.

Through many episodes like these I learned an important lesson about my friends: they accepted me for who I was. What a blessing it was to feel loved and cared about even with my obvious imperfections! Because of their acceptance, my friends helped me to accept myself. I learned that friends make it easier to get back up after we've fallen down, and start over again. Isn't that what friends are for? To love us and help us learn to better love ourselves? Good friends make all the difference.

Learning to cultivate true friendships is so important. We aren't meant to make it through our earthly journey alone. Heavenly Father often answers our prayers through those we are close to. We *need* friends. Even the Savior surrounded himself with those he called friends.

We must learn to discern true friends from false and to be a true friend to others. How are you at spotting a real friend from a phony? Let me share with you five prototype "friends." You decide whether someone you know fits the description. (You might even want to ponder whether you could be identified with one of our role models.)

First, there is Holly. Holly is a role player. She must be "in" at all costs. She seems confident but secretly seeks approval through sporting the "right" labels or linking herself to the latest hot fad. You must have these items, too, if you are to be her friend.

Then there is Polly. You have what she wants. She is your best friend when there is something in it for her. When her need for what you supply is gone, so is she.

Molly is the third "friend." This girl is a flake, but you can't help but like her, even though she doesn't know what *follow-through* means. She frequently cancels out on you at the last moment (when a better offer comes along), but she is such a flatterer that you just *have* to let her off the hook. Does the word *shallow* fit here?

Our friend Dolly dares you. If *she* is going to be involved in something, so should *you.* "Misery loves company" is a phrase that comes to mind.

Finally, there is Lolly—the one who dumps all her problems on you. Every day brings a new emergency. She would love to help you out sometime, but she's always too involved in her own difficulty of the moment.

Are there any changes you need to make in your circle of friends, or in your own attitude? Are you surrounding yourself with real friends, or have you become caught up in relationships that can go nowhere? As you learn to enjoy true friendships based on proper principles, you will find it easier to love yourself and easier to live the gospel. That's what friends are for—to help us learn to help ourselves.

From my own experience I have gained a greater understanding of the kind of relationship I should strive to obtain. I would like to share with you a few thoughts on seeking proper friendships.

You have heard this first thought tons of times, but I include it because it is mandatory for sharing real, lasting friendships. We must first *love ourselves*. Not a prideful, "me first" love, but a comfortable acceptance of who we are. Being able to look in the mirror and like who we see allows us to treat others in a positive way. When we feel good about ourselves, there is no need to tear another down.

You might want to try this simple experiment: Just for one day, vow to think only positive thoughts, about both yourself and others. If inadequacies or criticisms creep in, chase them away. Smile at people and say something positive. It might almost hurt to push those positive words out of your mouth, but do it! You'll feel better about everyone around you—and about yourself. We read that a friend esteems his *brother* as *himself* (see D&C 38:24).

Another important element in building true friendships is sharing your emotions. I've noticed that some people have a hard time with this. One friend of mine is a wonderful person, loaded with talent, fun, and sensitivity. I learned how difficult it is for him to show his tears, however, when a big group of us went to see the movie *Dead Poets' Society.*

Remember the very most intense part of that movie, when you wanted to bawl? The tears were dripping off my chin when my friend leaned over and whispered in my ear, "Hi! I'm Batman!" I turned to see him grinning and I wanted to kick him! He had ruined my moment! To break the tension, he had resorted to his own brand of humor. We laughed about that for a long time. The underlying thought here, though, is that often we *do* hold in feelings that would best be expressed. True friends share both happy times and sad times, knowing that strength comes from sharing. That's what friends are for—to share with and to grow with.

There are times when a sense of humor is the best thing to display. In fact, most of our relationships would benefit from having a healthy dose of laughter thrown in. Everybody loves to laugh. Have you ever gone to a movie and sat next to a guy who has a huge, hilarious laugh? Everyone is laughing, but not at the movie—at the *guy* who is laughing at the movie! Laughter is contagious and infectious and wonderful. We simply need to remember to laugh *with* others, not *at* others. A quick wit and a gentle sense of humor may turn a situation around for the better. Just watch the tension ease and a better spirit prevail when you learn to laugh. That's what friends should be able to do—lighten a load and lift a burden with a little smile, or a hearty laugh.

Remember the saying, "Practice Makes Perfect"? Another thing we may consider in cultivating true friendships is the need to practice being a good friend daily right in our own homes. Some homes are almost ideal, and others are much less so—but there is always room for improvement in the way we treat our family. These people should be our forever friends. Why is it that we ofttimes spend little effort in building our most precious friendships? After all, we never know how long they will be with us in mortality. It was from a friend I'll call Tina that I learned the importance of not storing up regrets for failure to build these friendships.

Tina is an average person who has good days and bad days. On one Saturday a couple of summers ago Tina had a *bad* day. Have you ever awakened in a *bad* mood? For no logical reason you're mad at the world and everyone in it? If so, you can relate to Tina. She stomped downstairs and announced that she was not going on the planned family picnic. Her mother gave her a hug and asked her to reconsider. Dad tried to make her laugh and cajole her into going along, but Tina would have no part of it. She was in a bad mood, after all, and she was going to enjoy it! Her brothers good-naturedly told her what a great day at the beach she was going to miss. When her baby sister toddled up and said, "Tina go wif us? I wuv Tina," she almost had to relent. But there was a principle involved here, and she wanted to "enjoy being mad."

Mom and Dad, sister and brothers, all took turns giving Tina a little hug or kiss before they laughingly went on their way to the beach, leaving a sulking Tina at home. Tina never saw them again. Their car collided with another, and all of them were killed instantly.

Can you imagine the feelings Tina experienced when she was told the news? What guilt she had to work through as she wrestled with questions like: "How could I have treated them so poorly?" "Why did I never get a chance to tell them I love them?" "Why did I take my anger out on them?" Tina felt she had waited too late to learn some important lessons.

We will never regret sharing loving, happy times with our

family. We will be better able to share loving friendships *outside* our family circle as we practice *within* our family circle. Even on our bad days, wouldn't we rather be remembered as the one who spoke kindly, and cared? Proverbs 17:17 tells us that "a friend loveth at all times."

The best way to discern a true friend, and to be one, is to focus on the One who is our truest friend—the Savior. He loves us deeply, and he has shown us by his own example the pattern we should follow for real friendship. A line of scripture reminds us that "thy friends do stand by thee" (D&C 121:9). It is during moments of great need that our truest friend always stands by us.

There will be times of despair, of heartache, for all of us. At these difficult times we may find our faith increase and our loving friendship with the Savior grow as we learn to know and trust him.

Let me share three short examples of how the Lord's friendship made all the difference during most difficult times. You may recall other stories you have heard and how they have caused your own faith to grow.

The first is of a little girl who was diagnosed with a fatal kidney ailment. She had spent many weeks in the hospital, only to have one kidney totally fail and the other quickly deteriorate. She was dying. The doctors told the little girl's parents she could leave the hospital so that her last days could be spent in the comfort of her own home.

But the child had been taught to pray, and the story went that she balled her little fists and fervently prayed with all her might that Heavenly Father would heal her and allow her to live. Several days passed, and the little one seemed much better. Upon examination and testing, the doctors were astounded to find two functioning kidneys!

The little girl learned at an early age that she had a true friend—one in whom she could trust.

The second story is of a relatively newly married young woman who was eager to have a family. After a miscarriage she was privileged to once again carry a child. For several months all went well—then she fell ill. The doctor who had seen her through her previous miscarriages gently took her hand and explained she had HELLP syndrome, which usually takes the life of the baby—and the mother as well.

The young woman was devastated. Shortly thereafter she was

given a blessing in which she was told that if she would trust her truest friend all would be well. Not too long after, she delivered a healthy baby girl. The young woman learned whom she could trust, and she understood the importance of accepting the Lord's love.

Now let me tell you of a woman busy with family, church, and community work. She seemed to lead a charmed life until she began experiencing head pain and ear problems. She went to a doctor, who sent her to another, who sent her to another. After running tests, the doctor bluntly told the woman she had either a certain disease or a brain tumor. A CAT scan was run to determine the exact cause. The results came back—it was positive for a tumor on the right side of the brain.

The woman "lost it" for a while. What would become of her family? How could she accomplish all she wanted to with such a short time left? Despair surrounded her. Finally, she received a priesthood blessing that told her the Lord loved her and considered her his friend; and that if she would exercise sufficient faith, all would be well. A repeat scan was done a short time after that administration. It revealed that where there had been a tumor, there was a blank space on the right side of the head. All was well! The woman learned whom she could trust. And she understood a little more about true friendship.

These stories are sacred to me, my young brothers and sisters. I was that little girl, and it was my parents who were told to take me home to die. I was that young woman so desperately wanting a child. The baby born to me is my daughter Andrea, now a vibrant, healthy teenager. And I was that busy mother who fell ill. I have seen the CAT scan reports that show where there was a tumor, and where there is now a blank space.

I have come to understand how much I must depend on the Lord, and how true *his* friendship is. It has taught me to appreciate the friendships I have been blessed with here. I have witnessed how our truest friend is there for us. I have experienced how he helps us learn to help *ourselves*, how he helps us learn to help *others*, and how he helps us learn to be our *best* selves.

Sometimes, during my less noble moments when I tend to be selfish or insensitive, I am quietly reminded of my Friend's sacrifice for me, of his loving assistance, and of his desire to have me likewise be a true friend to another.

Our *true* friends help us be the very best we can be. They are sensitive to our needs. They bring us closer to the Savior. They help us on our earthly journey as we move closer to our heavenly home.

And *that's* what friends are for.

Vickey Pahnke is a talented composer, writer, and recording artist. She is president of a production company and co-owner of a recording studio and serves on the board of directors for the Utah Special Olympics. She travels internationally presenting and performing for Positive Choices school programs. Vickey likes cooking, laughing, script writing, and watching old movies. She and her husband, Bob, live in Salt Lake City, Utah, and are the parents of four children.

CHAPTER 2

The Most Important Thing

Barbara Barrington Jones

Not too long ago, I was in Mexico with Elder and Sister Robert E. Wells giving firesides. I had learned to speak Spanish while growing up on the border in El Paso, Texas, and now I was having the chance to use that language as I gave my talks.

One morning I was sitting outside working on a talk I was to give for Education Days. I had been assigned the topic of keeping in tune with the Spirit. Elder Wells was sitting nearby, and I debated whether I should ask him for help. I finally decided to go over and bother him.

"I'm sorry to bother you," I said, "but I'm doing this talk on keeping in tune with the Spirit. Could you give me one or two little pointers?"

Elder Wells smiled and said: "You know, one time we had a meeting of General Authorities at which one of them gave his formula for keeping in tune with the Spirit. I don't think he'd mind if I shared it with you."

I was excited. A General Authority's formula! I had my paper and pencil ready to write. And what he said was so simple: "The key to all spirituality is the Savior. Fill your mind with thoughts of the Savior. Fill your heart with love for the Savior. Fill your life with service."

Elder Wells gave me some scripture references, then I went back to my chair and started thinking about what he had told me.

Fill Your Mind with Thoughts of the Savior

As I wrote the first step, my mind flashed back to the time when Sharlene Wells was in the Miss America pageant as Miss Utah. She told me that during the week's activities the contestants had to stand in alphabetical order by states, which meant that Sharlene was always next to Miss Texas. That year, Miss Texas was one of the favorite contestants. Sometimes the photographers would say things like, "Miss Utah, could you please move over so we can take some pictures of Miss Texas?"

The worst day was when each of the contestants had to have her picture taken sitting in the back of a convertible on the Boardwalk. When Miss Texas took her place it seemed that there were hundreds of flashes as photographers took her picture. But then Sharlene took her turn and climbed into the convertible. As she lifted her hand to wave, there wasn't a single flash. She was devastated. It all seemed so hopeless. What was she doing here? Why was she even trying?

More discouraged than she had ever been, Sharlene walked back into the hotel. But in this dark moment, Sharlene says, it suddenly came to her that the recognition from the world really wasn't important. It didn't matter. She had a wonderful family who loved and supported her. And she had the church that gave her a firm belief and knowledge of the Savior. At that moment she truly understood what was most important in her life—her knowledge of the Savior and his mission. Whether she won or lost in the contest just didn't matter.

Fill Your Heart with Love for the Savior

As I wrote down the second part of the formula I thought of another young lady. Her name was Christy Fitchner. She had joined the Church shortly before participating in the Miss USA pageant in 1985.

During the pageant she called me and said, "Barbara, I'm going home."

"What?" I answered. "The pageant isn't until tomorrow night."

Now, Christy is a beautiful girl, but she was terribly discouraged. She said: "I'm not as pretty as Miss California. I don't have as nice a wardrobe as Miss New York. I don't have as good hair as Miss Nebraska." She went through every state in the Union. She made the mistake of comparing herself to other people.

I told her: "Hang on. I'll be there tomorrow."

When I arrived, she was white as a sheet. Her chaperone told me she hadn't eaten in three days. I asked her if she would like a priesthood blessing and I finally found a bishop and his first counselor. A security guard showed us a little room we could use in the basement. It was a gross room with trash on the floor. I thought, "Oh, no, how can the Spirit ever be here?"

But when the two men placed their hands on her head the room seemed to disappear. I'll never forget the blessing Christy received. The bishop said: "Christy, your Heavenly Father is pleased with you, and he wants you to know that when you walk out on that stage tonight he promises to be there with you." The tears were just streaming down her cheeks. She stood up and hugged me and said, "It's not my problem any more."

When Christy walked out on the stage that night—talk about love! She radiated her love for the Savior. When you are filled with the Spirit, others can see it. It's the best beauty shop or source of self-esteem you'll ever find.

Fill Your Life with Service

The third part of the formula made me think of Gretchen Polhemus, Miss USA in 1989.

The first I knew of her was when Gretchen's father called me and asked if I would help his daughter. I usually only work with the state winners. I told him, "Well, she's not a state winner."

He said, "But you don't know my daughter. She's special."

Gretchen came to my house with beauty queens from Nevada and California. I didn't realize how much of a country girl she was.

I had the girls together for some training. I started at one end and said, "Now tell me, each one of you, what do you use on your hair?"

Gretchen said, "I go down to the feed store and I get something called Mane and Tail. I put that stuff on my hair, and it makes it so nice."

I tried to hide my surprise. "Oh, Mane and Tail, that sounds like a lovely beauty product."

The rest of the girls used normal things.

Then I asked, "Now, girls, what do you use on your fingernails?"

I started with Gretchen. She said, "I go down to the feed store and get a product called Hoof Alive. I rub that stuff on my fingernails, and it makes them hard, like horses' hooves."

All I could say was, "Oh, that's nice."

Then we talked about their pageant hairstyles. Gretchen said, "Oh, you're talking about that hairstyle that looked like I had a cow patty plopped right on top of my head."

I was thinking, "This girl really is from Texas."

We finished our training, and the girls were going to go down to Fisherman's Wharf, a fun tourist spot in San Francisco. Gretchen asked if she could stay with me.

I said, "Well, I'm doing a missionary zone conference, and you don't know what that is. You probably wouldn't like to go."

She just said that she would like to go with my husband and me.

We were a little late—you know Mormon Standard Time. Here were thirty-eight missionaries from the Santa Rosa Mission, and the zone conference had already started. I rushed up to the front and gave my talk. I finished, and then the missionaries started bearing their testimonies. As we were listening, Gretchen leaned over and whispered to me, "Can I go up there?"

I was amazed. "You want to go up there?"

She nodded.

I said, "Yes, it's okay."

She walked up to the front of the room. She had on a beautiful white dress with flowers all over it; she was in high heels with her hair up. Those missionaries had their mouths hanging open. She stood up in front of them and said: "I look out at all of you and am so proud of you. I never knew that this church existed until today. I'm just so proud of you that you're giving two years of your life to serve the Savior. You have been such an inspiration to me. I promise to be like you and dedicate my time to serving the Savior."

Now I want to let Gretchen tell you her own story:

"Do you believe that God has a plan for you? I do.

"The night I first competed for Miss Texas, I stood up there on the stage and the audience was in complete darkness. I had prepared and prayed to win, but I ended up second runnerup. I thought God had betrayed me. What went wrong? I wanted it for myself. I never bothered to ask if it was Heavenly Father's plan for me.

"The next year I told Heavenly Father that if he could use me more as Miss Texas than as just Gretchen, then I'd be Miss Texas. But if that was not in his plan, it would be fine. That night I walked out on stage, and I could see every face. I won and went on to win Miss USA. But I never had the feeling that 'I did it.' I wanted to follow Heavenly Father's plan for me, and this was part of it.

"I wondered how I was going to serve him for a whole year. He started to show me. Sometimes it isn't what you say that counts, it's how you act towards others. It's smiles. It's hugs. It's compliments. It's everything Christlike.

"I finished my year as Miss USA, and I started working for ESPN. And Barbara invited me to go with her on speaking assignments. Every time I would go with her into these church houses and to youth conferences I would feel something. I didn't know what it was, but it would make me cry. I had told the Lord that I would serve him, so I started speaking for a lot of other churches, but I never felt the same feeling there as I did in the LDS church.

"Barbara invited me to go to Japan to a big youth conference being held there, but she got sick and couldn't go. It's a fourteen-hour plane trip, and Brad Wilcox, another of the youth speakers, started telling me all about the Church. The neat thing was that nothing he said was scary to me. I was soaking it in all the way to Japan.

"At the end of the youth conference, before the testimony meeting, everyone sang, 'I Am a Child of God.' All these big tough football player-type guys with long hair and black T-shirts, they all sang. That really hit me. The Spirit was touching my heart. I saw something in those kids that I didn't have. I'd done a lot in my life, but I wanted to be like them. I sat back and cried. I knew then and there that someday I would be a Mormon. I just didn't know when. I thought, 'Heavenly Father, this is so special, so important, that it's taken me three years to know about this church. But if I join now, it will be just on emotion. I want to make sure that you tell me, and it's not me telling you when.' Brad encouraged me to keep praying.

"Back in the United States, I was going to meet Barbara in Provo, Utah, for a conference at BYU. As we were coming over the mountains into Utah Valley we dropped lower preparing for the long approach to the Salt Lake airport. I was looking out of the window. It was a beautiful sight, with the sun setting and the lights shining on the temple in Provo. I leaned against the window and said: 'Heavenly Father, I'm waiting on you. I know you want me to join, but I don't know when. I'm waiting on you.'

"I heard a deep voice say, 'Yes.' I turned around to see if someone was sitting behind me. There was a woman, and I knew she hadn't said anything. I thought, 'Was that me or was that Heavenly Father.' Then this sweet voice said, 'Come follow me. It's time.'

"I couldn't wait to tell Barbara."

When Gretchen got off the plane, she was so excited. She said, "Barbara, guess what!"

I said, "You're going to be baptized."

She said, "How did you know?"

I had known that if she would be open the Lord would literally guide her to the Church, the place where she can serve him the best.

I have to tell you another part to that story. When I got sick and wasn't able to go to Japan with the group that would be speaking, I was crushed. I just knew that Gretchen would learn so much, and I wanted to be there. But I just was too sick to go. Again, it was part of God's plan.

I had met a girl named Dede Day in Washington state two years before. She was a nonmember, but had been invited to sing at a women's conference I had been asked to speak at. She was interested in participating in a pageant, so I told her I would like to work with her. I didn't hear from her for two years. She called just before I was to go to Japan, and I had to turn her down. But when I became ill, I called her and invited her to come for some training.

We started working on the winning formula—preparing all areas of your life, and letting Heavenly Father's plan work in your life. She was willing to let the Lord guide her life. She went home and won her pageant.

I invited her to participate in a program I was giving. She was going to sing with Kenneth Cope, a popular LDS speaker and performer. They were practicing in a room in my house. I was standing in the doorway, listening to them sing, and I had a premonition that he would baptize Dede. I pulled Kenneth aside and told him, and he brushed it off a little.

We were taking Kenneth to the airport, and he started giving Dede some heavy-duty discussions of doctrine. He started bearing his testimony to her. When he told her about the preexistence, the tears just started rolling down her cheeks.

Kenneth said, "Oh, did I offend you?"

Dede answered, "No. I already know. I've known all my life."

Then he said, "We believe in a prophet of God."

And she said: "I know. All my life I have had these feelings of how things were. I just felt it. I knew there had to be a prophet. God isn't going to leave us now. All these things, that God and Jesus Christ have bodies, and that they and the Holy Ghost are all separate. I knew it. I just kept it to myself. Faith was about the only thing that my mother and I never discussed. We talked about everything else. But when I heard you telling me everything, I just knew it was true."

When Dede went home she talked to her mother in general terms about being baptized. Her mother said it was her own decision. She said to her mother: "You know, Mom, nothing is going wrong in my life. I just won my pageant. Everything is going great. Why do I feel so empty inside? It's like there is something missing in my life. I just feel so lost."

Dede came with me to a youth conference. It was the first time she had heard people bearing their testimonies. As we left, she turned to me and said, "Barbara, I just want to thank you for bringing me here. I'm not lost anymore."

When Dede got on the plane to go home she had a tape of Kenneth's songs she was learning. One song came on, and the words said: "He lives again for me. He said, 'Come follow me.'"

Dede said: "It hit me hard. It was a burning feeling. I couldn't hold back the tears. I just looked up and said, 'Okay.' And I heard a voice say again, 'Come follow me.' Christ was telling me right then and there what I should do."

Dede was baptized the same day as Gretchen.

So what is the most important thing? I'm going to let Gretchen tell you.

"I wish young people knew that if they would live like they are supposed to, staying close to the Savior, they can have anything they want provided it's Heavenly Father's will. I learned that Heavenly Father does want us to work for things. If they are righteous desires and we present them to him and say, 'This is what I want. Now, is this what you want for me?' He will guide us."

I know that there isn't one girl or young man out there that isn't loved and cherished by our Heavenly Father. He gave each of you talents and abilities, maybe more than you even suspect. You have to do your part, prepare, practice, and work. And search for ways to use them. Then wonderful things will happen to you, wonderful things that Heavenly Father has in his plan for you.

Barbara Barrington Jones, an image consultant, grooms young women for beauty pageants. She likes walking, healthy foods, working with youth, and writing books. A world traveler, she has been a fashion designer/coordinator, modeling school owner, and classical ballet dancer. She says, "The greatest event in my life was finding Christ in this church." Barbara and her husband, Hal, have two children.

CHAPTER 3

Win
from Within

Suzanne L. Hansen

Has science pegged you yet? Nearly forty thousand studies on human nature are published every year by psychologists, sociologists, and pollsters. They find out incredible things—like what girls and boys like to talk about.

The studies have discovered such things as that girls talk far more than boys about family, weight, health, and clothing. Imagine that! And boys talk far more than girls about sports, food, news, music, and cars. And girls and boys talk equally about work, movies, and TV. Have I written anything that surprises you, yet?

It may sound as if I'm poking a little fun at one of the studies. Just a little. But several other studies and stories show us the dramatic results of mental toughness in young people and others. I think we tell ourselves that success is just for the lucky, the smart, the good-looking, or the rich. Actually, success comes to those who know how to *win from within.*

Here are four steps to help you unleash that vast goodness and greatness inside and overcome obstacles and problems.

1: Just Go for It

During the 1990 Wimbleton Tennis Tournament sixteen-year-old Yugoslav Monica Seles faced American Zina Garrison. As the tennis match progressed it became very clear that Seles's most formidable opponent was not Garrison but herself.

"The match was very close," said a sad Seles afterwards. "I was going for all the *safe* shots. Even on Zina's second serve I was really scared to hit the ball for winners."

Garrison, on the other hand, didn't play it *safe*. "I just told myself to go for it," she said. "None of this tentative stuff. If I missed, at least I'd know that this time I really went for it—wholeheartedly."

Zina won—from within. But in 1991, guess who won Wimbleton. Right! Monica Seles would not be denied again. She had learned the importance of winning from within.

One study showed that most people in tough and difficult situations usually play it safe. We should ask ourselves the question: Rather than going for it, do we concentrate on minimizing our losses rather than on winning?

At school, if a particular test score of yours is low, do you automatically think you're dumb—do you peg yourself a "failure" and "hex" yourself for failure on the next test? "I just don't get this," you may chide yourself. Or do you think: "This is just one setback. I know I can do better, and I will!"

Remember: You are the sum total of what you make up your mind that you are. Just go for the *win*. Don't worry about failure.

2: Make Up Your Mind to Be Happy— No Matter What Happens

Thomas Edison's manufacturing facilities were heavily damaged by a fire one night in December 1914. Edison lost almost one million dollars' worth of equipment—a huge loss, even by today's standards. Also lost were the records of much of his life's work. How overwhelming this must have been for him! Everything he had hoped and dreamed for was gone.

The next morning, as he walked through the ashes, the sixty-seven-year-old inventor said: "There is value in disaster. All our mistakes are burned up. Now we can start anew." Edison understood the great principle of remaining optimistic and cheerful in the face of problems.

Things may not be perfect for you. You may have made mistakes in your life—we all do. And sometimes bad things happen to us that are totally out of our control. But remember, tough-minded optimists approach problems as learning experiences and thus grow stronger within.

The Lord has counseled us, "men are, that they might have joy" (2 Nephi 2:25). Even though we are in a world full of problems, studies show that upbeat, happy people do better in school, are healthier, and even live longer, than pessimists.

So how do I become happy with problems? Look for the good. Abraham Lincoln said that we are about as happy as we make up our minds to be.

If you aren't feeling happy or successful, look down deep inside yourself. That's where it all starts. I truly believe that you are a child of God with great abilities, gifts, and talents waiting to be unleashed.

3: Rehearse Success

Winners always picture or visualize themselves accomplishing their goals. But in the face of hard times it's a little more difficult for some to see opportunity and success—as Davy Hair did.

On Father's Day 1978 this brawny eighteen-year-old was working as a life guard at a swimming pool in Fairfield, New Jersey. Suddenly, amidst the fun-filled sounds of swimming children, came a shrill cry for help.

Davy's heart started to pound in anticipation. He looked quickly around and spotted a child struggling in the deep end and crying for help. Davy reacted quickly and dived off the nine-foot life-guard stand into the pool.

The next thing Davy saw was a white flash as his head struck the concrete bottom of the pool. The water turned red around him, and Davy felt himself starting to slip away. Then he felt someone pull him to the surface. It was his brother, Brian.

Davy muttered over and over, "There's someone in trouble, there's someone in trouble." "Don't worry," Brian said. And then came those penetrating words. "The kid was faking it."

Davy's neck was broken. He had irreversible spinal damage.

He was paralyzed. The next day Davy spent three hours in surgery. The doctors rebuilt his shattered neck, taking bone from his hip to do so.

"Let me die," became Davy's cry. He had had everything before. Six-foot-four, 220 pounds, blonde hair, blue eyes, a leader, tons of friends, a passion for sports and a love of life—now flat on his back, unable even to feed himself. What did life have to offer?

Davy thought of suicide, but he wasn't even capable of doing that. Then one day he looked at his loving family who were continually by his side. He looked at his brother, Brian, who had saved his life and who kept telling Davy that he could beat this. Davy decided then that he owed it to them to at least give life a try. With that decision he had started on the road of winning from within.

After many months in the hospital and many difficult therapy sessions, Davy had regained the use of his upper body. He announced to his mother: "A wheelchair is not important. I used to walk from one place to another. Now I go on wheels. What's important is what I do when I get there."

Six months after the accident Davy moved home and started school again. He began swimming and lifting weights. One of his teachers suggested he enter wheelchair track events. He pictured himself entering races and winning, and hurling the shot long distances. But disappointment after disappointment came. However, he did not give up.

In 1979 Davy won a bronze medal in the shot put at a wheelchair track event. There he met the world champion wheelchair athlete, whose muscular chest and arms and powerful throws astonished him.

Davy made up his mind that he was going to beat that guy. Over and over in his mind he rehearsed pulling up to the mark and hurling way beyond the champion's throw. He even saw the crowd going crazy.

Davy's training now began in earnest. At seven o'clock each morning Brian helped him stretch his arms. Afterwards he swam half a mile and then worked out for two hours on a weight-training machine over his bed. With this strenuous regime he increased his strength till he was able to bench press four hundred pounds and his biceps bulged to $18^{1}/_{2}$ inches. In 1982 Davy won three gold medals at the World Games, beating the champion. The moment he had rehearsed in his mind for three years had happened. In 1985 he graduated from law school and picked up three more gold medals at the National Wheelchair Games.

Davy occasionally recalls those days of despair in the hospital. "I remember thinking," he says, "that one day I would stand at the gates of heaven and God would ask what I did with my life. And I would respond that I broke my neck, so I didn't have to do anything."

Sure, the neck could have become an excuse. But Davy stopped concentrating on what he couldn't do and rehearsed over and over in his mind success and winning. And that's what happened.

And that's what can happen for you, if you also take the fourth step in the face of your challenges.

4: Don't Lose Your Cool—No Matter What

A nurse is trained to keep her cool, especially in life-threatening situations. But it might be different if a personal disaster occurred. This happened to critical care nurse Katie Kemble. She kept her cool and saved her own life.

On Saturday, 27 May 1989, Katie and Ric Hatch were rock climbing on a beautiful, warm day near Grand Junction, Colorado. Katie was waiting on the ground, while Ric was starting to climb. Suddenly Ric yelled a warning: "Rock! Rock!"

Katie jerked to attention to see Ric flatten himself against the granite cliff to avoid the boulders the size of trash cans that came crashing down the mountain and exploding all around Katie. She started to run, but a boulder ricocheted off another rock and slammed into the back of her left leg. The force of the blow tossed her five feet into the air as blood sprayed all around her. She landed on the spur of a jagged stone and felt scalding, ripping pain engulf her.

Glancing down she could only see two splintered bones protruding below her left knee. Half her leg was missing!

Ric quickly descended while Katie looked around for the rest of her leg. She found it lying close to the left of her body, still attached at the knee by an inch-wide band of skin and muscle. Suddenly, Katie realized that she could die from this. As a nurse, she knew she could bleed to death in a matter of minutes from an open leg artery.

She put the thought aside, and focused on how to stay alive. She had been trained to control her emotions and face her fear. Now it meant her very life. She said to herself, "You know what to do, now do it."

Ric's face said it all when he hurried over to her. She immediately started to reassure him by giving him detailed instructions and tasks to do. To their relief, they discovered that the artery had been pinched when the leg was severed, so the bleeding was not as severe as Katie had first thought. They wrapped the stump with a jacket, and Katie carefully held her leg so as not to further tear the one-inch band of tissue. Then Ric picked Katie up and started with great difficulty down the steep trail.

At every step Katie was racked with pain, but she kept encouraging Ric, telling him exactly what to do if she should pass out. Finally they staggered off the trail and saw another climber who had witnessed the rock slide and was there with his truck. Ric lifted Katie into the back of the truck. Forcing pain from her mind, Katie carefully straightened out the almost severed limb.

Ric cradled her in his arms as they sped down the road. Bumps sent bolts of pain through Katie's body, but she concentrated on keeping her leg in alignment so the tissue wouldn't tear. She forced herself to keep alert. She knew she was the only one with a medical background and she had to stay conscious.

When she got to the ranger's station, there were only newly trained volunteers there who had never seen a worse injury. She saw their ashen faces so she took command. "I'm a critical care nurse. You've got to start an IV." She thrust out both fists, clenched to expose the veins. "Use a 16 gauge needle and run in lactated ringers as fast as you can. You've got to take my blood pressure every five minutes."

Katie's knowledge and presence of mind impressed everyone, and they jumped to action. Within the hour Katie was stabilized. Soon a life flight helicopter took her to St. Mary's hospital. Katie's desperate need to direct her own rescue was over. She had made it.

Both sections of the leg had repairable arteries. This was a miracle. She had a chance of using that leg again. She had dug down deep inside and found the power to focus on overcoming the odds. If she had lost her cool she might even have lost her life.

How many of us keep our cool when we are bugged by family members or others or have problems eating at us. The power is in us to overcome all odds against us. Our very eternal lives are at stake. The Book of Mormon says, "Counsel with the Lord in all thy doings, and he will direct thee for good" (Alma 37:37). But we can only hear his counsel if we are calm and quiet inside.

That's it. Four steps to winning from within. (1) Just go for it by not fearing failure. (2) Make up your mind to be happy. (3) Rehearse success over and over in your mind. And (4) Keep your cool—no matter what.

Nancye Sims wrote a beautiful poem, "There Is a Winner Inside Each of Us."

There Is a Winner Inside Each of Us

Winners take chances.
Like everyone else, they fear failing,
  but they refuse to let fear control them.
Winners don't give up.
When life gets rough, they hang in
  until the going gets better.
Winners are flexible.
They realize there is more than one way
  and are willing to try others.
Winners know they are not perfect.
They respect their weaknesses
  while making the most of their strengths.
Winners fall, but they don't stay down.
They stubbornly refuse to let a fall
  keep them from climbing.
Winners don't blame fate for their failures
  nor luck for their successes.
Winners accept responsibility for their lives.
Winners are positive thinkers
  who see good in all things.
From the ordinary, they make the extraordinary.
Winners believe in the path they have chosen
  even when it's hard,
    even when others can't see where they are going.
Winners are patient.
They know a goal is only as worthy
  as the effort that's required to achieve it.

                      (Nancye Sims)

Winning from within is not something I dreamed up. It's the Lord's plan for all of us. Success is an inside job. He tells us that if we search diligently, pray always, walk uprightly, and be believing all things will work together for our good (see D&C 90:24).

Stubbornly believe that the best is yet to come.

Suzanne L. Hansen, author of five books and a lecturer and businesswoman in Salt Lake City, was college homecoming queen and in 1980 and 1981 was named one of the Outstanding Young Women in America. Arts and crafts, flower arranging, classical music, and new age music are included in her list of favorite things. Suzanne and her husband, Michael, have three children.

CHAPTER 4

Getting Along, Getting Even, or Getting Out? Loving When It's Hard to Love

Mark Ellison

Let's get a move on, Elder!" I yelled at my lazy missionary companion. Fully dressed in my crisp, new navy blue suit, scriptures in hand, name tag in place, I was ready and eagerly waiting to venture forth from our humble little missionary apartment and preach repentance to the wicked world outside.

My slowpoke companion, however, was still shaving. I paced back and forth in our miniature living room. It was so small that you couldn't pace far. One or two steps in one direction, that was it; then you had to turn. Pace, pace, pace. I waited, then yelled again: "Come on, Elder Raymond!"

"Keep yer shirt on, El-durr!" he hollered back in his Ozark mountain drawl.

"That's my companion," I thought, as I resumed my pacing. "My lazy, ball-and-chain, sloth-of-a-missionary companion. Great! I get a burnt-out, trunky, about-to-go-home Elder for my first companion in the mission field." I grew red with frustration. Mission rules said we had to be out of our apartment and busy at our missionary labors by nine-thirty each morning. I looked down at my watch. It was ten-forty-seven. I decided it was time to yell again. "It's no wonder we don't have any investigators to teach!"

"Hey!" Elder Raymond's mousey little face, half-covered with shaving cream, appeared in the bathroom doorway. "Put a lid on it, Ellison."

It's kind of funny now to look back on the difficulty I had in getting along with Elder Raymond, but at the time there was nothing funny about it. There I was, on my *mission*, the experience that was supposed to be the spiritual pinnacle of my life thus far, and I was having these terrible feelings of impatience and anger!

I had never even imagined that my mission would contain the possibility of such contention. But the life-style sure was challenging. I was never to leave the presence of my companion. The first thing I'd see in the morning and the last thing I'd see at night was his face. I'd hear his singing, listen to his dumb jokes and the stories about his family, eat his cooking, and see all his weaknesses. He and I seemed totally different: I was raised in the fast-paced subculture of southern California, and he was raised in the hillbilly lands of Missouri. I talked fast, he talked slow.

As the weeks went by, our missionary work seemed to drag. I mean, it was *slow*—I mean slower than cold molasses trying to drip uphill in January. We couldn't seem to find *anyone* interested in talking with us. As we encountered disappointment after disappointment I became convinced that it was all Elder Raymond's fault. *He* was the slow one. I began to miss home, family, girls, my truck, and my guitar. Soon I had developed a truly spectacular case of homesickness, and that too was his fault, I felt. I began to hate my companion. And guess what happened to the Spirit in our missionary work! It left. Now, that's no way for a missionary to live.

A terrible, dark feeling accompanies contention. It is the opposite of the love, peace, and joy which accompany the Spirit of the Lord. "The Spirit of contention is not of me," said the Savior, "but is of the devil, who is the father of contention, and he stirreth up the hearts of men to contend with anger, one with another" (3 Nephi 11:29).

What should we do when we have a hard time getting along with someone? Elder Richard L. Evans used to say, "Anyone can get along with perfect people, but our task is to get along with imperfect people." I think the Lord understood that we would sometimes have difficulty in doing that. Nevertheless he instructed us, "Love your enemies." Now, how do you love someone you can't stand, or who can't stand you? Well, the Lord gave us some ideas as he further instructed us: "*Bless them* that curse you, *do good to them* that hate you, and *pray for them* which despitefully use you, and persecute you" (Matthew 5:44, emphasis added).

One morning, while Elder Raymond was showering, I sat on my bed reading the scriptures. Actually, I was reading *a* scripture, the same verse, over and over—not because it was especially inspiring, but because I couldn't concentrate; I had to keep thinking, "Where was I?" and start reading over again. I couldn't concentrate because out of the corner of my eye I could see Elder Raymond's messy bed. I knew it would take him forever to make his bed, get dressed, and be ready to go, and the very thought had me fuming. I yelled toward the bathroom, "Elder, how long are you going to be?" No answer.

Finally, I put my scriptures down, stomped over to my companion's bed, and made it for him—fluffed up the pillow, tucked in the sheets, the works. Then I sat back down on my bed and returned to my reading. I could finally concentrate.

A few minutes later a bathrobe-clad Elder Raymond walked in. He stood in the doorway, looking at the room, perplexed. I pretended not to notice. "Say, El-durr," he drawled, "di' joo make mah behhd?"

I decided to play innocent. "Why no, Elder, but it looks really good. Just a sec—I'm almost done with this chapter—and then I'll join you for companion prayer."

"Now, hold on," Elder Raymond muttered, his brow furrowed in thought. "Ah know *Ah* didn't make mah behhd, and . . . thar's just yew and me here . . . *yew* must've made mah bed!"

Well, now you know I was wrong when I said my companion was slow.

"No, really," I insisted. I was beginning to have fun with this. "It must have been someone else." Then I smiled, "Maybe an angel came down and did it."

That really cracked up Elder Raymond. "An angel, eh? Har, har, har!"

The next morning, as Elder Raymond showered, I quickly made his bed for him again—big, fluffy pillow; nice, tight hospital corners, the way my Mom had taught me; I could have bounced a quarter three feet off the covers, no fooling. Then I sat on my bed, read my scriptures, and tried not to laugh. Moments later, in walked my companion. "Say, El-durr, joo make mah behhd agin?"

"It wasn't me, Elder, honest."

"Looks lahk that *angel* come back agin, eh?"

"Yeah, must've been The Angel."

Once again, this struck him as being absolutely hilarious. "Har, har, har, har!"

The Angel struck every morning for a week, and then one morning Elder Raymond said to me, with a half-suppressed grin, "Say, El-durr, why don't yew go shower first today?" I did, and as I came back into the bedroom a few minutes later I noticed that *my* bed had been made! The pillow was fluffed up, the sheets tucked in neatly. Elder Raymond sat on his bed, pretending to be engrossed in the scriptures. I smiled and asked, "Say, El-durr, *joo make mah behhd?*"

He laughed and said, "Musta been that *angel* agin!"

Well, from that time on Elder Raymond and I began to do nice things for each other, and we'd usually blame them on The Mysterious Elusive Angel. I discovered that my companion had a good sense of humor! We began to enjoy each other's company, and to sing together as we worked. It lifted our spirits and made our days happier. I no longer hated my companion. I *liked* him—really, truly, genuinely liked him. And I liked being a missionary again. And guess what happened to the Spirit in our companionship! It came back.

We began to have good experiences talking with people about the gospel. I learned many things from Elder Raymond about how to teach and converse with people. We saw some of our investigators enter the waters of baptism and make covenants with their Father in Heaven, and join the church of his son Jesus Christ. We shared many spiritual experiences.

I'll never forget the day when we knocked on the door of a lady who was in terrible pain with a back injury. We taught her about priesthood blessings. Elder Raymond and I laid our hands on her head and blessed her by the power of the Melchizedek Priesthood. The influence of the Spirit was powerful as my good companion boldly declared that this lady's pain would subside immediately. After the blessing, the lady stood with eyes wide and wondering, and quietly spoke: "My pain is gone." Elder Raymond and I testified that we were representatives of the church that held the power and authority of God, and the lady said, "Thank God for young men like you, who go about in the world doing good." And you know what? I began to love my companion. I loved Elder Raymond.

Elder Marvin J. Ashton has stated that we serve that which we love (see *Ensign*, May 1981, p. 22). Conversely, it is also true that we come to love that which we serve. So love those you don't get along with; but if you find that difficult, bless them, do good to them, and pray for them until you *do* love them.

How well do you get along with those in your family? The story is told that one Monday night a Latter-day Saint family gathered together for family home evening. The father taught the lesson that night. He began, "Okay, family—let's each try to name one of the Ten Commandments!" Little Timmy said, "Thou shalt not steal!" Mary Sue and Betsy said "Keep the Sabbath Day holy" and "Don't take the name of the Lord in vain." Then it was the turn of Tom, the teenage son. "Um, honor thy father and thy mother."

"Fine," the father said with a smile. "Now, for the next week we're going to try our hardest to strictly obey the one commandment we've each named, and next week on family night we'll each report on how well we did!"

Right away, Teenage Tom raised his hand. "Uh, I'd like to change my commandment, please."

His father groaned and said, "Well, okay smarty, which commandment would you like?"

Tom came back quickly, "Thou shalt not kill."

Would you agree that it's generally easier to go a week without murdering than to go a week honoring your parents perfectly? Getting along with parents and other family members is a common difficulty for young people. Some of that tension may be normal and natural, but much of it isn't. What effect does it have on your life if there are bad feelings between you and others in your family? Well, the Holy Spirit will not be where there is the spirit of contention. And if we need anything in these times we live in, we need the companionship of the Holy Spirit!

I once asked some of my students in seminary to think back to their most recent good, spiritual experience—maybe it was while praying or reading the scriptures, or maybe it was in a testimony meeting or a class at church. Can you recall your most recent spiritual "high"? Now think forward from that time—eventually you came down from off that spiritual peak. We all do. That's natural. But was there something that *prematurely* brought you down?

As I asked my class this question many of them raised their

hands and shared what had happened. One by one, each student related that he or she had been *invaded* spiritually by contention in the home: "My parents were fighting." "My brother was being a nerd, and I yelled at him." "I heard an angry heavy metal song on my stereo and the Spirit left." "My sisters were spreading rumors about me at school." "My Mom and I had an argument."

If you are involved in contention within your home, my heart goes out to you. I realize it may not even be your fault. May I share some advice with you? First, if there are disagreements, talk them over without shouting, for "a soft answer turneth away wrath" (Proverbs 15:1). Don't fall into the habit of "getting even" with others in your family. If someone has hurt you and you decide to "get even" by hurting back, you have only "gotten even" by lowering yourself to the other person's standard. Be *above* getting revenge. Instead of making things worse, make things better by following what the Savior said. *You* initiate the change, whether the contention is your fault or not. That's the Christian thing to do. Remember what the Apostle John said about Jesus: "We love him, because he first loved us" (1 John 4:19).

I know of a young lady who was raised in a home where she was ridiculed and tormented by her father. He had wanted a son, and since a daughter wasn't to his satisfaction he made her life miserable. She grew up and moved away, but she found herself consumed by bitterness and hatred toward her father. She spoke to her bishop about her troubled background, and to her surprise the bishop said to her: "The day you ask your father to forgive you for the bad feelings you've had about him will be the day you receive peace to your soul."

The young lady stared at her bishop and said: "No, you don't understand! *He's* the one that should be asking *me* for forgiveness!"

But the bishop calmly reaffirmed: "No, *you* don't understand. The day *you* ask him to forgive *you* for the bad feelings you've had about him will be the day you find peace."

She thought about that, and the next time she was home for vacation she approached her father. In a trembling voice she said: "Father, I know we didn't get along well, and I've felt very angry towards you for that. I want to tell you I'm sorry for the way I've felt, and I ask your forgiveness."

The father hung his head in shame and then slowly looked up.

There were tears in his eyes. Finally, he said, "No, my child—*I'm* the one who should be asking you to forgive *me* for how badly I have treated you. I'm so sorry."

That conversation was a healing moment in their relationship, and it happened because the young lady took the initiative to make things right. She could have rationalized, "I'm out of the house now, I'm on my own—why try to make things better?" But she made the effort, and peace came into her life. Don't fall into the trap of merely *putting up with* a bad situation until you're old enough to "get out." I don't think that's what is meant by "enduring to the end."

Cherish your family. As the unknown author of the following thought suggests, you may not even realize yet just what an important part of your life those loved ones are:

4 years: My daddy can do anything.
7 years: My dad knows a lot, a whole lot.
8 years: My father doesn't quite know everything.
12 years: Oh well, naturally Father doesn't know everything.
14 years: Father? Hopelessly old-fashioned.
21 years: Oh, that man is out of date. What did you expect?
25 years: He knows a little bit about it, but not much.
30 years: Must find out what Dad thinks about it.
35 years: A little patience, let's get Dad's meaning first.
50 years: What would Dad have thought about it?
60 years: My dad knew literally everything.
65 years: I wish I could talk it over with Dad once more.

We don't have to be thirty years old before we learn to appreciate each other. I know many terrific young Latter-day Saints who openly love and get along with their families, and their lives are stronger and happier for it. Yet I also know some—too many—for whom my heart aches because their dearest relationships are tainted with anger or bitterness.

I bear you my testimony that the key to our peace and happiness is living the way taught by Jesus Christ. He is "the way, the truth, and the life" (John 14:6); the Savior, the Healer, the Prince of Peace. There is enough mercy in one of his tears to drown a lifetime of sorrows. There is enough power in a minute of his love to wash away the ugliness of years of contention. And there is enough virtue in his miraculous atonement to bring us home, if we are worthy, to the eternal family of our Heavenly Father, where joy, peace, and love abound.

Mark Ellison is a seminary instructor in Springville, Utah, and is a part-time American sign language teacher at Brigham Young University. He has served as a director of Especially for Deaf Youth. Mark enjoys triathlon racing, and he feels that youth have an incredible potential to change the world around them. He and his wife, Lauren, are the parents of two children.

CHAPTER 5

If You Only Knew

Steve James

The new school year had just begun. I was a junior in high school, and my sister was a freshman. We both were looking forward to a great year in seminary. I was excited because I could be an example to my little sister and show her how incredibly intelligent I was.

On the first day of school, at 6:00 A.M., we arrived at the church and entered the classroom. Our teacher began to ask some questions so he could see how much we knew about the year's theme. I answered his first question. My sister was impressed. After several other questions, he asked, "Who were the two people who assisted Joseph Smith in translating the Book of Mormon?" Immediately my sister's hand went up. I thought to myself, "This is not a freshman level question." There was silence in the classroom and all eyes were focused on my sister. Somehow I could hear the faint echo of Jeopardy music in the distance. The teacher repeated his question, and my sister blurted out, "Urim and Thummim!"

Sometimes we think we know the answers to so many questions when in reality we don't. I would now like to ask each one of you one simple question. Who are you? I'm not asking you what your name is or what's on your driver's license (if you have one). I'm asking if you really know who you are as a spiritual child of our Heavenly Father.

When I was fourteen, my greatest desire in life was to be a rock star. I became a professional entertainer and performed all over California with various musical groups and bands. I thought that fame and fortune was the peak of anything I could ever achieve in life. I remember, as my older friends began to leave on missions, thinking that just maybe I could serve my "mission" in the world of pop music. Of course, it was only a dream, but one that was real to me.

By the time I turned sixteen my family had relocated to Salt Lake City, Utah (the entertainment capital of the world!). I continued to entertain throughout the area as I finished my years in high school. I remember too that during the summers my friend and I would climb up on his roof at night and talk about girls, church, and basketball. I never really could play basketball, but we talked about it anyway. One particular night we were both silently staring at the stars. I thought to myself, "All I can see is a bunch of stars in the sky." (I was an intelligent sixteen-year-old.) I seriously wondered if anyone was out there. During my whole life I had been taught that there was a God, but for a split second I questioned his existence. I wanted to know if he was there, if he listened to my prayers and knew the secret feelings of my heart. I had always believed in him, but I just didn't know if my testimony was based on my parents' teachings or on my own personal knowledge.

I decided to go home and find out for myself. I figured that if Joseph Smith could receive an answer to his prayers at age fourteen, after reading the passage in James 1:5, "If any of you lack wisdom, let him ask of God," then I could also receive my own answer. That scripture applied to me too. I went home and prayed. I was hoping that somehow I would receive a glorious answer through some miraculous experience. But instead, I felt nothing.

I continued my prayers over the next couple of days. I felt that the Lord must have been testing me to see if I really had the desire to obtain a personal testimony. Finally it came. I received my answer. Not in some dramatic way, but rather through a sure yet indescribable feeling that came to my heart. I knew for myself that God did exist and that I was his child. I could feel that he loved me and that he knew me—better than I knew myself. I also had the feeling that he had many things in store for me. I wondered if that would include being a rock star.

Before I knew it I was nineteen years old. I hadn't reached the heights of stardom, so I decided to go on a mission and put my career on hold. As I completed my mission papers I thought of the many places where I could be called. I kind of hoped that I would be sent to the Hollywood California Mission, or the New York City-Broadway Mission, where I could find some record producer. As I sang at his baptism he would say something like, "That voice!" just as one would picture in a movie. He would then offer me a record contract and I would be a rock star.

My call came. The moment I had anticipated finally arrived. "You are hereby called . . . to labor in the Costa Rica San Jose Mission." What excitement! A foreign country! My first verbal reaction was, "Dad, where's Costa Rica?" My mom then exclaimed, "It's next to Nicaragua, where there's a war!" (That was a "mother" thing to say.) I thought to myself, "Spanish . . . I can barely speak English!" Yet I had a peaceful feeling inside my heart that Costa Rica was where Heavenly Father wanted me to go. I soon found out that my mission also included the country of Panama. I accepted the call with great enthusiasm.

A few months later I found myself walking down the streets of Panama City with my new companion. We were on our way to an appointment we had made with a lady named Anna, her sister, and her son. It was my turn to give the third discussion in Spanish, something I had never done before. I was petrified. Being a "greenie" (a new missionary), I could barely speak the language. We entered the small apartment, where Anna welcomed us, and sat down on two worn, dusty chairs.

My companion opened the discussion and then turned to me and said, "Elder, le toca," which means "your turn." My teeth began to chatter, and not because it was cold—after all, I was in Panama City. I nervously began the discussion, "En el año de 1820, había un joven que se llamaba José Smith . . . ," when all of a sudden I felt a shower of feeling spread throughout my entire body. Tears came to my eyes as I thought of the great prophet, Joseph Smith. I knew that he was a prophet and that I was so privileged to be carrying the message of the restored gospel to these humble people.

As I finished, I looked at Anna and her sister. They were crying. I looked at my companion who had tears in his eyes. Now, that scared me! What did I say? What had I done? My companion proceeded to give the baptismal challenge. I thought to myself, "That's not supposed to come until another discussion!" And then they said the one Spanish word I did recognize—"Si." Yes! I was so excited!

When we returned home my companion sat me down on the couch and asked me what had happened. I simply repeated the experience I had had and then asked him why he was so concerned. He told me that as I began to teach about Joseph Smith my voice changed, and I began to speak fluent Spanish, just like a Latin. I knew then that Heavenly Father had provided a miracle so that Anna and her family could understand the message of the gospel.

They were baptized two weeks later. From that experience I learned that I was nothing without the Lord; and more important, that there was something much greater than being a rock star. It was to be an instrument in the hands of the Lord.

A few months later I received a new companion, an elder from Honduras. I think I liked him so much because he was shorter than I was. He looked a bit like Sammy Davis Jr. and was missing his two front teeth, so he spoke with a lisp. Needless to say, it was difficult to understand him. He could barely understand my broken Spanish, so we often travelled in either silence or confusion.

One afternoon we were walking down the sidewalk of Panama City's famous Balboa Avenue, taking a short cut toward a neighborhood where we had an appointment. All of a sudden I felt an inner voice saying, "Turn back." I thought I was crazy, and I continued with my clueless companion. The feeling returned, this time even stronger. Then it came again a third time. I turned around and started running. My poor companion didn't know what was going on but he followed me, blurting out something in Spanish.

When I reached the sidewalk, my companion caught up to me and asked in a puzzled voice, "What are you doing?" I answered in confusion, "I don't know!" At that point I observed a lady walking down the street with two boys, one on each side. They were coming toward me. The feeling returned. "Talk to her." "No," I said to myself, "I'm not in the social mood right now." Have you ever had a feeling to talk to someone about the Church and you're afraid of what that person is going to think? That's the way I felt. In addition to that, I didn't know if she would even be able to understand my attempt at speaking her language.

The feeling once again came back as my hand went out to shake hers. "Hola," I said, "yo soy misionero de La Iglesia." (In English), "Hello, I'm a missionary from The Church . . . ". She interrupted as tears surfaced in her tired eyes. "I've been waiting for you to come to me for three years now," she cried. The following week, she and five of her children were baptized. I learned that as the Lord's instruments, we must worthily follow the Spirit.

Toward the end of my mission I served in an area in Costa Rica called Desamparados. One day I was exploring a new street with my companion when we both had a distinct feeling to visit a certain house. We knocked on the door. It opened. We found the sweetest middle-aged woman on the other side, who invited us to come in. She accepted our challenge to listen to the discussions and invited us to return.

Over a period of two months my companion and I taught her every discussion and made many friendly visits. But after one particular visit she announced to us that she was content with her religion and that we were only welcome to return as friends, not as missionaries. We were walking out of the door when a voice came from the back of the house saying, "Mom, can I listen to what they have to say?" It was her eighteen-year-old son. She replied, "Well, yes, if you want to, Eddie."

Eddie came out from the shadows of the hall. His eyes seemed to sparkle. He was the kind of person missionaries pray to find. We taught him for six weeks or so. Finally, during a discussion, I asked Eddie if he had prayed to know whether the things we had taught him were true. He replied, "Well, more or less." He said that he had little privacy because he shared a room with his brothers. He told us that he had once felt that he was getting an answer, but he was interrupted. I told him, "Eddie, I would give anything so that you could know that these things are true. I would even give my life."

I couldn't believe what I had just said! I quickly bore my testimony, we ended with a prayer, and we left. I had just told someone I would give my life for him. I didn't know if I really would. My heart was beating faster and faster as I approached the house where missionaries had lived for years. There I knelt beside my bed and began to literally cry to my Heavenly Father. I wanted to know if I really would give my life for Eddie, for anyone, for Him.

The answer came to my heart clearly, yet so peacefully. I wasn't required to die. But what Heavenly Father did expect of me was to give of the life that I'm living. I then understood. Heavenly Father gave us life, and the greatest gift that we can offer him is to give our own lives by serving him. I asked him to answer Eddie's prayers.

The next time I saw Eddie, I was walking down the street. His face seemed to glow as he turned around and saw the two of us coming. I knew he had received his answer. He asked if he could be baptized the following Saturday. Then he began to sob as he told us that he would be disowned by his father for joining the Church. Eddie chose to give up the life he knew in order to follow the Savior.

I'm so grateful to have served a full-time mission. Because of those two years I know more about the spiritual "me" and my purpose here on earth. Although I had many trying experiences, the principles I learned through that service will in turn serve me for the rest of my life. When we are in the service of the Lord we find ourselves, our spiritual identities. I am so thankful to all those elders, sisters, and senior couples who selflessly serve as full-time missionaries all over the world. Young men, let me ask you, is it so much of a sacrifice to give two years to your Heavenly Father, who gave you life in the first place? Young women, what a blessing it is for you to also have that opportunity to serve, if you desire. The Lord needs all of you. I would hate to think what would have happened to Eddie, to Anna and her family, to anyone I taught during my mission, if I had decided not to go.

I'm thankful for my personal testimony that came to me at a young age. What a blessing it is to know that we are of divine inheritance, of infinite worth; that we are children of God. So many leaders have called the youth of today a "chosen generation." You are some of the greatest spirits ever to exist, reserved for these last days to come to earth and accomplish many great things. If you only knew who you really are as spiritual children of God, I think you would change the way you are living. You would look to the Lord in every thought and surround yourself with uplifting people and circumstances.

> If you only knew who you are,
> Why you've been placed here on this earth to live,
> Taken from your home so far away.
> Do you remember then?
> If you only knew how great the love

Your Father feels for you within his heart.
He's waiting from his throne above.
You promised him that you'd return
To live with him for all eternity.

If you only knew who's watching over you
With blessings from those realms on high
That we seldom see and recognize.
Oh, why are we so blind?
If you only knew what lies in store for you
As you face your life ahead.
Remember, long ago you said
You'd follow him every day.
You promised him you'd never stray.

If you could only recall the spirit that you were,
And promises you made back then.
If you could only see your Father's loving face
And look into his eyes again.
Would you change the way you live
And love enough to give?
What would you do
If you only knew?

If you only knew how great the pain
Your brother suffered long ago.
He died for you, but not in vain.
Will you remember him?
If you'd only do
What you've been called to do.
If you only knew.

Being a musician, I play several instruments, one of which is the piano. I am its master. I can play whatever I want to when I want to. But no matter how skilled I am, if the instrument is out of tune the song just won't sound the way it was intended.

We are instruments. The Lord is our Master. But are we in tune? We are a symphony of instruments that together can play a miraculous melody under the direction of the Master. May we always keep ourselves in tune. May we remember who we are.

It is my prayer that we will all return someday to our Heavenly Father and live in his kingdom forever. For he is our Father and we are his children. And it is my further prayer that when we are there we will be able to kneel at the feet of our elder brother, he who gave his life for us, and be able to say that we have given our lives to him.

Steve James is a professional entertainer, song-writer, and motivational youth speaker living in Provo, Utah. Vice-president of a busy production company, he has addressed youth groups across the nation representing many anti-drug and anti-substance-abuse organizations. He has also been involved in organizing benefit concerts for the Special Olympics. Steve enjoys going to the beach, hiking in the mountains, and traveling to new places (including Japan, where he spent five weeks performing on tour).

CHAPTER 6

I Will Overcome

Stephen Jason Hall

After a depressing day at school, where my once-high spirits had been stomped on by every passerby, I felt I needed a pick-me-up. The greatest boost I could find was the grounds of the Provo Temple. Often I would go to the temple to enjoy the beauty of the grounds and partake of the spirit that resides in a place so close to the Lord's heart. This always seemed to lift my spirits. On this occasion, with my spirit healed and my vision renewed, I headed home.

On my way I encountered a group of about ten children, all around the age of six. Instantly I was surrounded by this legion of the curious who buried me in a throng of questions. "How do you drive that?" "How fast does it go?" and "Can I try?" they asked as their eyes danced with excitement. I did my best to suppress their hunger for knowledge by taking each on his own ride on what they perceived as the ultimate of go-carts.

During this time I noticed one of the children, a little Polynesian boy, who was more interested in just looking at me than asking questions. He circled me over and over, each time paying special attention to the sides of my head. With each pass an intent look of concentration grew across his face. After about ten minutes he stopped, and stood square and confident, directly in front of me. Then ever so tactfully he imparted the results of his careful study. "Hey!" he yelled, demanding my attention, "You got big ears . . . like a monkey!"

I couldn't believe it! As I turned back towards the temple to find refuge from this peewee bully, I asked, "What's your name?" And as poised as ever, he announced, "Hickey." Suddenly I didn't feel so bad.

Adversity is something that we all encounter almost daily, so none of us need any familiarizing with it. In fact, each of us has an experience something like this one of mine every day of our lives. We encounter people who remind us of our imperfections; or, more often, we remind ourselves. So regardless of the specifics of our trials, adversity is a part of everyday life. None of us would even try to debate that. The question then becomes, "How can we overcome?"

After a diving accident that left me paralyzed from the chest down, I spent over a year in and out of different hospitals and therapeutic institutions, for seven weeks of which I was unable to move or speak. Now, when you can't move and you can't speak, you have a lot of time to think. It was in these few mute and motionless weeks that I learned some of the valuable lessons of my life. Most important, I found that although none of us has exactly the same adversity as someone else, the ways we overcome are similar and can be applied across the board. And I'd like to share some of those ways with you.

First, I'd like you to pause for a minute to reflect on your life. Take a few seconds to complete a short activity. Find a piece of paper and write down the first five things that come into your mind for which you are most grateful. When you have completed that, on the same piece of paper write down your number one adversity, the mountain that you are climbing currently. When you have done that, hold on to the paper. We will refer to it later.

I believe there are three essential elements in our quest to overcome. If we apply them properly we will find the energy to conquer.

Faith

Faith is first, because without faith in the Lord and in the gospel as a base the other two concepts don't mean very much.

As I returned home from the hospital I began to integrate myself back into the rigor and life-style of the tenth grade. I started with just two classes, really taxing ones: choir and seminary! I went mostly to get into the social scene. This plan was a good one, for many of the high school kids were totally unaware of my situation and I needed to know how to help them understand.

I remember one day especially. I was in the seminary class, sitting by a girl (girls are the kind of people I usually like to sit by), when my leg had a muscle spasm and began to tap up and down on the footrest of my wheelchair. When my leg has a muscle spasm it looks very natural, very real, almost as if I have control over the movement, but in reality I don't. It is totally reflex, and I have as much control over it as someone does over the jerk your leg makes when the doctor hits you in the knee—that is, none.

My friend Nicole, however, wasn't aware of this condition, and as my leg began to tap, her eyes got as big as silver dollars. She jumped out of her chair and yelled, "He's healed!" I thought, "Oh, no!" The whole class turned around, ecstatic, and started to do the dance of healing. I couldn't believe it! Finally the whole class calmed down and the situation was explained. Of course, as you might imagine, they were so embarrassed. I personally thought it was the funniest thing I had ever seen, and I laughed myself all the way home.

Once home, I reflected on the experience and marveled. What was it that made my friend believe that right there in class, within the twinkling of an eye, I could be totally and completely healed. I believe it was faith.

I think about faith often—about what it is and how mine might grow. I believe that faith consists of two parts, belief and action. Alone they are useful, but together they yield power. Belief alone can do many wonderful things. There is a warm feeling and a sense of peace that comes with believing in gospel truth. Action also can stand on its own with great merit; many of the wrongs of the world have been righted by virtuous action. But when the two are united, belief and action, they produce power— the power to overcome.

I know it is through this power that we can overcome the trials we experience in our daily lives. I know that as I believe in the gospel, in its principles, in my Father in Heaven, and as I act on those beliefs, the day will come, whether in this life or the next, that I will stand from my wheelchair, hold it over my head, throw it as far as I can, and run until I drop—or, if it is in the next life, do some equivalent jubilant action. I know that day is in my future, and as surely as I know that I know too that as you increase in your belief and act upon your belief a similar day awaits you. Then you can rid yourselves of the adversities that have for so long held you down and you can find the freedom you have always prayed for. I find great power in this thought.

A Thankful Heart

I woke up especially early that mid-September morning, for my mind was particularly full. September had been an unusually hard month for me. Three hundred and fifty miles northwest from Salt Lake City, in Boise, all of my classmates had started high school and were enjoying all the joys that accompany it. While they attended football games and pep rallies (not to mention those senior cheerleaders), I was stuck in a hospital waiting for my daily meds. This state of mind easily allowed me to focus on what I didn't have.

I especially concentrated on the paralysis of my hands and all of the things I could not do because of that paralysis. Nightly I would pray that I might regain the use of my hands. It did not seem too much to ask; I figured I had been a good kid, I did not really deserve a crippling handicap. And I became altogether sure that if this partial healing took place I could then be happy. I began to spend all my time concentrating on all the things that I would be able to do if I only had use of this faculty. It seemed such a simple act for a God who created the worlds, and I knew that with the use of my hands I could lead a normal and happy life. In short, I could live as a paraplegic but not as a quadriplegic.

Luckily, even in the face of such an attitude I had resolved that in my daily therapy I would give everything I had. Hours upon hours I exercised, stretching and pulling, doing everything in my power to strengthen my remaining muscles. It was hard, but the time went quickly enough, and my daily progress made it all worth it—until Dan came.

Dan had been in an accident similar to mine and it caused his spine to be damaged and paralysis to ensue. But he had escaped with total use of his hands and partial use of his legs. He was part of a world that I could only dream of joining. Yet he would sit there the entire therapy hour whining and complaining that he was unable to totally use his legs. "Today, lets concentrate on your upper body," the therapist would plead daily, only to hear Dan's all-too-familiar response: "I just wish I could move my legs. Maybe this is the day I'll be able to walk." And there he'd sit for the rest of the period, thinking about his legs, watching them for movement, rarely lifting an arm or pushing a weight.

This frustrated me no end. "You fool!" I thought. "You idiot! Don't you see what you have? Just look at all the blessings and opportunities that are yours simply because you can move your hands. You have access to a freedom that I pray for, and you are too wrapped up in your own self-pity to see it."

One night I found myself in the room of my friend, Rich Hullinger. I had noticed that Rich constantly wore leather braces on his wrists and hands. Near the beginning of my hospital stay I had worn similar braces in order to stretch my tendons, but it seemed odd that he would still be wearing them. That night I asked Rich about them. He explained to me that the break in his neck was one pinhead higher than mine, and that because of that he was unable to move his wrist up and down, or even hold it straight against the power of gravity.

I returned to my room and prepared for bed. I didn't sleep much that night; over and over I thought of how blessed I was that I could make that simple movement. Suddenly, I found within my own persona everything I hated in Dan. During the past few days I had spent the bulk of my time concentrating on what I didn't have, when I could have been focusing on what I *did* have. Centering my efforts on wishing I had different circumstances, I had become totally oblivious of the many blessings in my life. This oblivion had caused my outlook on life to become tarnished. It affected the way I dealt with others; my zeal for life; and most important, the way I felt about myself. However, with this new re-alization of how much I did have, and how much I had taken for granted, I began to feel more blessed. As I felt more blessed, I be-came more thankful. And as I became more thankful, I developed a sense of worth, which brought a newfound ability to overcome.

Sometimes we get so caught up in wanting the green grass that's on the other side that we overlook the greatest blessings right before our eyes. One of those overlooked blessings is the mountains we are called to climb. Do you find blessings in your adversities? Refer to the list you prepared at the beginning of this chapter. Is your trial on the list of things you are thankful for? I know that if it is, or if it ends up there, you will find new strength and ability to overcome. This paralysis has been the hardest thing that I have ever had to deal with in the entire twenty-one years that I have spent on this earth, but it has also been the source of the greatest blessing, insight, and growth during those same twenty-one years. Each time I find my mountain unbearable I remember that, and this gives me the inspiration to carry on, the ability to overcome.

Enduring to the End

After being released from the hospital, for the first few months I was without the aid of a powerdrive wheelchair. This was OK as long as I was on hard surfaces like wood or tile or linoleum. But if you put me on carpet of any height or texture, I was dead in the water. One particular autumn day, the builders who were redoing our home to make its facilities accessible to me were getting the final measurements for my bathroom. I went in to make sure that the sink, shower, and toilet would all be the right height for me. I loved to be in the bathroom because of its tile floors, so I was pushing all over the place. I went over to the sink and then to the toilet, then over to the shower and back to the sink, just burnin' up that ol' tile floor; a regular Mario Andretti.

When the measurements were all taken down, Dad waved the checkered flag signalling that it was time to go, and I headed toward the bathroom door. As I reached the portal I felt a sudden jerk that threw me and my wheelchair back into the confines of the bathroom. Baffled by this unexpected opposition, I looked down to see what gigantic boulder, rolled automobile, or dead body had halted my forward progression. My investigation ended with some pretty disappointing results, for the only possible culprit I could see was a little tiny gold threshold about one quarter of a centimeter high, almost flush with the carpet. I could not believe that such a small obstacle had halted the greatest speedster that bathroom tile had ever known.

Knowing how the incident frustrated me, and loving a challenge as he does, my dad took a twenty out of his wallet and laid it on the floor. That was all the motivation I needed. I was fifteen years old—I'd sell my sister for twenty bucks. Summoning every bit of strength I had, I pushed with all my might toward the evil doorway. Upon my arrival the previous result was repeated, and I was thrown back into the bathroom. Another twenty went on the ground. Again I tried, and again I was unsuccessful. Another twenty. Again I strenuously pushed, and again I was foiled. Another twenty. This continued until there were five twenties on the ground—*one hundred dollars!* Over and over I tried, grunting and sweating, giving everything I had, but to no avail; always I found myself in what had become the depressing confines of my new tiled-floor bathroom.

Seeing that I had lost this battle in the war, my dad picked up the money, came over to me, put his arm around me, looked me lovingly in the eyes, put the bills back in his pocket, and encouraged me to keep trying. In the end that advice has proved to be of more worth to me than piles of twenties. I kept trying, every day for the next month getting my brothers and sister to put me in the bathroom so that I might fight my way out. Finally, thirty days after my first attempt, my front wheels passed the threshold and my back wheels followed. I had overcome! My arms flew in the air as if I was an Olympic champion. I *felt* like a champion. There was no crowd chanting my name and no national press to take my picture for their front page. The hundred dollars was long gone and spent. But all this didn't matter. I had persisted and conquered, and the joy of it was sweet.

I believe we can relate this experience to the life of every one of us. We can all come to possess this same kind of feeling as in our daily lives we hold on during both good and bad times, overcome by faith (see D&C 76:53) and effort, and thus endure to the end as the Lord has instructed us to do.

I know that The Church of Jesus Christ of Latter-day Saints is the one true and living church. I know that God lives and that he loves us. The Book of Mormon is his word translated by his servant Joseph Smith under divine direction. I know that Joseph was the mouthpiece of the Lord and spoke His words. I know that President Ezra Taft Benson does the same today. I also know that as I increase in my faith, always possess a thankful heart, and endure to the end, with the Lord's help I *will* overcome!

Stephen Jason Hall, a student at Brigham Young University, grew up in Idaho. He enjoys music, plays, public speaking, basketball, and BYU football. An Eagle Scout, while in high school Jason was junior class president, community education coach, and member of the seminary council. At BYU he has been an executive director in student government and a member of the Honor Code Committee, and was recently elected Student Body President.

CHAPTER 7

And They Tell Two Friends, and so on, and so on: The Damaging Effect of Gossip

John G. Bytheway

A few months ago a young friend of mine called and wanted some help. She was miserable, embarrassed, and almost without hope. Rumors were being spread that were causing her to lose friends and lose sleep. She was doing her best to live her standards, and people were calling her "stuck up." How could they be so mean? And how should she respond? We talked for some time and tried to figure out the best way to react or endure.

I have another friend I'll call Allison. Allison's life was nearly destroyed by gossip. Rumors accusing her of being loose and immoral raced through her school. She eventually had to change schools to escape from the effects. The saddest part of this story is that many of those who pushed Allison away were in her own ward. She felt humiliated at church and embarrassed at school.

It seems that each of us, whether as participants or as victims, have been mixed up in gossip. Gossiping is mean. It's worse than mean, it's evil. It hurts.

You've probably guessed by now that this chapter is about gossiping. You're right. But I hope it's more than that. President Benson once said: "The Lord works from the inside out. The world works from the outside in. . . . The world would mold men by changing their environment. Christ changes men, who then change their environment." (*Ensign*, November 1985, p. 6.) Saying only "Don't gossip" is an outside-in approach—change the outside (your behavior), and perhaps the inside will change too. The *gospel* approach is different. Change yourself *from the inside-out*, then temptations, such as gossiping, will be seen for what they truly are. The inside-out approach examines not your behavior but your identity, your mission, and your responsibility. When you truly understand yourself on the inside it will show in your behavior on the outside. Obedience will become a quest instead of an irritation. Let me see if I can illustrate what I mean.

Imagine yourself alone on the bleachers in a spacious basketball arena. Emerging from a dim hallway leading to the court is the silhouette of a tall, athletic man. He is wearing a red jersey that says "Bulls."

You know who he is, and with anticipation you run out to meet him. A basketball is sitting on the court, so you pick it up, run to him, and say: "Michael Jordan, I've always wanted to meet you! You do things on the court that make my jaw drop. You blow me away!" Your nervous hands throw him the ball, and you say, "Do that 'Air' thing!"

He is slow in his response. He looks puzzled and answers quietly, "What?"

"You're . . . you're Michael Jordan! I watch you all the time! You're one of the greatest basketball players ever!" He still looks confused, and you're becoming frustrated. Does he have amnesia? He has no clue who he is and what he is capable of doing.

"Wake up, dude, you're Michael Jordan . . . Earth calling Jordan . . . Are you 'Air' Jordan or 'Airhead' Jordan? Come on!" But it seems that no amount of effort on your part can convince him of his real identity. Once more you try to tell him, and he looks down and says, "I can't do this, I can't play basketball . . . " And he walks away.

If you're reading with your spiritual eyes and listening with your spiritual ears you probably understand the analogy I'm trying to make. How many time have prophets and Apostles tried to tell *you* who *you* are, and why *you* are here? When will your spirit awaken? Do you recognize the tugging inside?

To quote President Benson again: "For nearly six thousand years, God has held you in reserve to make your appearance in the final days before the Second Coming. Every previous gospel dispensation has drifted into apostasy, but ours will not. . . . God has saved for the final inning some of his strongest children, who will help bear off the kingdom triumphantly. And that is where you come in, for you are the generation that must be prepared to meet your God. . . . Make no mistake about it—you are a marked generation." (*Ensign*, November 1989, p. 36.)

You might want to read that quote again. President Benson recognizes you. He knows who you are, and he calls you one of "God's strongest children." Knowing this, you can see that to ask you to stop gossiping or to be nice isn't nearly enough. That's the outside-in approach. It's far more important than that. He's asking you to make a major change in your whole understanding of who you are. That's the gospel way—inside-out.

The fact that you are reading this right now says something about your true identity. In the premortal life you prepared yourself and became valiant. Imagine what a tragedy it is if, after being sent to earth with such a bright and brilliant mission, one of "God's strongest children" chooses instead to get his or her hands dirty with activities that are destructive and low. If someone with such potential chooses, for instance, the filthy, ugly work of gossip. It would be like going to the basketball arena to see Michael Jordan and finding him dozing in a back alley, being a bum. Wouldn't you think it was a terrible waste if you saw "Air Jordan," with all his talent and ability, drunk and sleeping in the gutter?

Anyway, before we go on and talk about gossip, I wanted you to get a sense of who you are and why you're here. Perhaps you don't play basketball, but you do have amazing talent and ability. Whatever your particular mission, it has nothing to do with something as low as gossip.

The rumors about my friend Allison resulted in many tears and much heartache. As I listened to her tell her story, I thought about the little poem we used to hear, "Sticks and Stones." The last part says "names can never hurt me." I began to wonder if that was really true, or if it was just an ideal we were shooting for.

> Sticks and stones can break my bones, but names can never hurt me.
> But oh, the hurt I feel inside when friends I've known desert me!
> For now I'm left to walk the crowded halls of school alone,
> And wonder what's been said today, when the whispering is done.

And when I kneel to pray at night, I shed a little tear
And ask for Heavenly Father's love, and trust He will be near.
Now, if you want to break some bones, some sticks and
    stones will do,
But if you want to break a heart, just spread a lie or two.
'Cause sticks and stones may break some bones, but broken
    bones can mend,
But spread around an evil fib, and the hurt may never end.

When the woman taken in adultery was brought before Jesus, her accusers referred him to the old law which said that such offenders should be stoned. Today, we view that kind of punishment as terribly brutal. We wonder how anyone with any compassion could throw stones at someone until they were so beaten, bruised, and bloody that they died.

Gossiping is like mentally stoning someone. A person can be torn, bruised, and bloody on the inside without having a mark on her physical body. Those with real compassion won't throw physical or mental stones. Once mental stones are thrown, or once thoughtless words are spoken, they cannot be recalled.

Boys flying kites haul in their white-winged birds;
You can call back your kites, but you can't call back your
    words.
"Careful with fire" is good advice, we know;
"Careful with words" is ten times doubly so.
Thoughts unexpressed will often fall back dead.
But God Himself can't kill them, once they are said!

(Will Carleton, *The First Settler's Story*, as cited in *Ensign*, November 1987, pp. 16-17.)

Some may ask: "Is it still gossip if it's true? How can it be bad to talk about it if it's the truth?" Again we can look at the example of Jesus. It is clear that the woman brought to him *was* taken in adultery. The accusations made against her *were* true. So how did Jesus respond? "He that is without sin among you, let him first cast a stone at her. . . . And they which heard it, being convicted by their own conscience, went out one by one, beginning at the eldest, even unto the last: and Jesus was left alone, and the woman standing in the midst." (John 8:7, 9.)

Once again, the issue is not whether the gossip is true. We all

make mistakes, and we could supply others with plenty of ammu-
nition to stone us (that's why we have the saying, "Those who
live in glass houses shouldn't throw stones"). The real issue is
contained in the questions: Why are we here? Is it our assignment to hurt people? Are we here to "confess" others' sins, or our
own?

Being critical of others, even if we feel justified, damages *our*
spirits, dulls *our* spiritual sensitivity. Elder Dallin H. Oaks said,
"The primary reason we are commanded to avoid criticism is to
preserve our own spiritual well-being, not to protect the person
whom we would criticize" (*Ensign*, February 1987, p. 68).

As a youth you have major decisions to make in the near future: decisions about your mission, your marriage, and your education. No doubt you will need the guidance of the Holy Ghost in
making those decisions, so you can't afford to decrease your ability to feel its influence.

As you grow older and more mature you will often wonder
where you stand with the Lord. You'll wonder if you're making
any progress. One way you can tell whether you're growing spiritually is the way you view other people. The Prophet said: "The
nearer we get to our heavenly Father, the more we are disposed
to look with compassion on perishing souls; we feel that we want
to take them upon our shoulders, and cast their sins behind our
backs" (*Teachings of the Prophet Joseph Smith*, p. 241).

When we see someone with a problem, what is our first reaction? Do we begin to criticize in our minds? Or do we feel sympa-
thy and wish we could help? A person who is growing spiritually
will immediately feel compassion. He will not want to publish the
problems of others; instead he will want to take those problems
and make them his own.

So far, we've looked mostly at participating in gossip. But
what if you've been a victim of gossip? How do you deal with it? I
asked for some ideas from a good friend who works with youth
every day. She wrote a letter about her own experience with gossip. I was amazed at what I read. She had been through some very
difficult times, but she handled it so well that you'd never know.
Here's part of her letter:

"I feel now, looking back, that the thing I probably needed the
most was for someone to reach out and listen, or help me to feel
accepted somehow. I didn't receive those things from my family

and I was never a good student, so I really didn't feel it at school either. I was different than the other kids at church and school.

"Anyway, I liked one of the guys in my ward and he started liking me. The problem was that his girlfriend was also in the ward. I couldn't date, so we could never do anything together, but we talked on the phone a lot and we talked at church.

"He was the one that finally told me about what not only the girls were saying but what the boys were saying! Some of them I didn't even know. I mean, I knew who they were but that was about it. I'm still not accepted into that group; to this day they talk about me and treat me weird . . . mean, really.

"I can't tell you how many times I would cry, at school, at home, at night before I went to sleep. I felt like the people that knew the gospel would be the ones who would be understanding—but honestly they were the worst. When I felt like I was in honest need, no one seemed to be there. Confusing, huh?

"One lesson I learned then was that even though people can be un-Christlike, you can make even that kind of situation a positive one.

"I didn't have anyone else to depend on but my Heavenly Father. So whenever I was sad or lonely I prayed and talked to God. I would never change my relationship with him, and those are the years the foundation was laid.

"Another thing was that I learned not to care what anyone else thought of me. God and myself were the only ones that mattered.

"The other thing was this: people show what shepherd they follow by the things they say and do. People talk a lot about intentions, and I believe if someone has honestly good intentions their actions and words *follow*. We talk a lot about commandments and living them and their importance, when we can't even be nice to others.

"I love my Father in Heaven; he helped me through that experience. I learned that my testimony, although young, was centered on the Savior, not on the people in the Church.

"One last thing I learned. Harboring bad feelings towards the girls in my ward was like poison. It hurt me, and I became more like them than I wanted to. Just like any poison, it destroys more than it does good—I had to give up the bad feelings to get rid of the poison.

"I still hate gossip. I think it's so evil because it's so hard to replace self-esteem when it's lost. People have the power when we're weak to take it away, but only we have the power to give it back."

This young woman handled these trials well. She drew *closer* to God instead of further away, and she eventually learned to forgive. She knew that Heavenly Father and one other person makes a family—and that family saw her through.

She could have held onto a grudge, but she learned that holding onto bad feelings is like poison, and she let them go. When you feel that your life and your reputation have been destroyed it may be a hard thing to accept, but you must learn to forgive. "Wherefore, I say unto you, that ye ought to forgive one another; for he that forgiveth not his brother his trespasses standeth condemned before the Lord; for there remaineth in him the greater sin. I, the Lord, will forgive whom I will forgive, but of you it is required to forgive all men." (D&C 64:9-10.)

Some are criticized because they are trying to hold on to their standards. It's common for people to become uncomfortable when they see someone who lives what he or she believes—perhaps it makes them evaluate their own life, and they feel they've fallen short. If they're insecure, they may begin to gossip. The first young friend I referred to was labeled as stuck up. All she could do was be herself, try not to judge others, and remember deep inside that God knew her, and he knew her heart. "Blessed are they which are persecuted for righteousness' sake: for theirs is the kingdom of heaven. Blessed are ye, when men shall revile you, and persecute you, and shall say all manner of evil against you falsely, for my sake. Rejoice, and be exceeding glad: for great is your reward in heaven: for so persecuted they the prophets which were before you." (Matthew 5:10-12.)

One of the most difficult things in life is to be accused of doing something wrong when in fact you're trying to do something right. It happened to Jesus all the time. It happened to Joseph Smith. It happened to a chief judge named Pahoran (if you want to see a classy reaction to a false accusation, read Alma 60 and 61). It happens to many people. If it happens to you, you might be tempted to run out and deny everything and try to set the record straight. But often that can make things even worse. Instead, just be yourself. Go out and quietly live your life in the best way you know how, and eventually the rumors will become harder and harder for people to believe. In any case, God knows you, and he knows your heart, and his opinion of you is the only one you have to be concerned with.

Of the many gospel topics and gospel principles this chapter could have covered, this chapter was about gossip. But I hope it was more about you—from the inside-out. President Harold B. Lee called the youth of today the most "illustrious spirits born into the world in any age of mortality." You don't need to gossip. It is a dirty business far beneath you and your potential.

May you catch this vision and always be found doing the noble work of standing for the right, building your fellowman, and preparing for that day when our Savior will come again.

John G. Bytheway, an administrator in Continuing Education at Brigham Young University, is currently working on a master's degree in Instructional Science. His interests include running, reading, playing the guitar, and all kinds of airplanes and cars. John's suggestions to youth are, "There is life after high school; and your experience there is not a forecast for the rest of your life."

CHAPTER 8

Broken Arms, Broken Hearts, and Confession

Brad Wilcox

Everybody make a human pyramid," I called out. It was a large youth gathering. I was helping with some mingling activities and games. "Come on," I cheered, "You can do it."

The groups quickly started piling up. Those on bottom rows pretended not to be in pain. The young people were involved, enthusiastic, and perhaps a little too competitive.

One young man, seeing that his group was falling behind, decided that the best way he could help them was to slow down the group next door. He playfully ran up to the almost completed pyramid and kicked the arm of the boy on the end of the bottom row. Science textbooks say that gravity is a law. Suddenly, twelve teenage bodies obeyed the law and came crashing down on top of one teenage arm.

With no time to lose, I packed the poor victim into my car and rushed him to the hospital, where doctors examined him. The young man listened bravely as they explained everything they would have to do to fix his broken arm. The hospital was busy. The process was drawn out. We went from admitting room to X-ray room to casting room to examination room, waiting in each place as though we were in line for the main attraction at Disneyland.

I felt sorry for my young friend. He had planned to spend his evening at a dance. He had anticipated a night of food, females, and fun. Instead he spent the whole time alone in a hospital with Brother Wilcox.

"So, how many in your family?" I tried to get a conversation started. Along with family, I asked him about his interests and mission plans. We spoke of seminary, sports, school, Scouts, and scriptures. We shared our favorite foods, books, hobbies, and finally, gospel principles. "I think one of my favorites is repentance," I said. "I'm so thankful Christ has given us the chance to change our lives and be better."

Suddenly, my friend became quiet.

In a movie script, this would have been a great time for the doctor to enter. But this wasn't a movie. No doctor came. Finally my friend spoke. "Brother Wilcox, what if someone has done something in the past that he's not really . . . " He paused. "Well, I know you're going to say go see the bishop, but that's the problem. I really can't go talk to him, because he thinks I'm such a good kid, and I don't know how telling him this stuff can help anyway. I would rather that no one ever knew about it."

I had come to the hospital with a young man in urgent need of attention for a broken arm. Now I realized there was a broken heart that needed attention as well. I tried to grasp the teaching moment and asked: "What should someone do if he breaks an arm? Now, I know you're going to say that he should go to the hospital and see the doctor, but that's the problem. The doctor might think he hurt himself. And I don't know how telling a doctor can help a broken arm anyway. Maybe the guy should just go around with his arm broken in five places, feeling severe pain, and not tell anyone."

"Okay, I get the point," my friend admitted. "But I really don't even know where to start."

During the rest of the evening, in between X-rays and casts, we talked about the what, who, when, where, why, and how of confession.

What is confession? Confession is the full, complete disclosing and honest telling of our sins to someone else. It is an important and necessary part of the repentance process. In the Old Testament we read, "He that covereth his sins shall not prosper; but whoso confesseth and forsaketh them shall have mercy" (Proverbs 28:13). In the current dispensation the Lord said, "I . . . forgive sins unto those who confess their sins" (D&C 64:7).

Who hears my confession? In scriptures we are told of three parties to whom we confess: God (Psalm 32:5), his authorized representative (Mosiah 26:29; D&C 58:17-18; 59:12), and, when necessary, to the person we have offended or injured (D&C 42:88, 92).

Many young people willingly take care of the first. In private prayer they openly confess all to their Heavenly Father. It's talking to his authorized representative, the bishop, that gets tricky. "I don't think my bishop will understand," some might say. Actually, they'll be surprised at how sensitive, loving, and caring their bishops will be. "But I'm too embarrassed to tell him what I've done," I have been told by others. "He'll be ashamed of me and think I'm totally evil or kinky." Young people with such concerns have, as the Lord says, "feared man and have not relied on me for strength as [they] ought" (D&C 30:1). We must remember that what God thinks of us matters much more than what a bishop might or might not think.

"Well, can't I just talk to my Young Women leader or my friends?" some ask. Disclosing our problems and discussing innermost feelings are essential to emotional healing and good mental health. But proper confession is more than simply unloading excess baggage. If disclosure were the entire purpose of confession, we could bare our souls to anyone on the street and be done with the matter. Confession, as a part of repentance, involves more.

Many in the world see the value of private meditation. Casual onlookers might mistake a Latter-day Saint's prayers for mere meditation. But although they may appear similar externally, we know that prayer is much more than meditation. In the same way, confession, as part of repentance, involves more than merely talking with someone, even with a psychologist, counselor, or big sister. We must see the bishop. This is the Lord's way.

Some might ask, "Are you saying that I should never talk to a friend or a trusted adult?" Not at all. You may talk to whomever you wish. But you would be wise to be careful who you take deeply into your confidence, for obvious reasons. (If the problem must ultimately have the bishop's attention, why risk possible future embarrassment by sharing it with friends other than parents?) Elder Vaughn J. Featherstone teaches that a "third party" (a person other than an immediate family member or the bishop) can have a "tremendous influence for good in a youth relationship" (*A Generation of Excellence* [Salt Lake City: Bookcraft,

1975], p. 168). However, if I wish to borrow my father's car, telling my desire to every person I come in contact with doesn't get me to the end I want. Others can understand, feel sorry for me, and even prove to be a great help and support, but ultimately my Dad is the only one who has the keys I seek.

In exactly the same way, when it comes to confession, the bishop is the one with the keys. He is authorized by Christ and the Church to help us get to the end we truly desire. Elder Boyd K. Packer affirms: "There is a great cleansing power. And . . . you can be clean. . . . For those of you inside the Church there is a way, not entirely painless, but certainly possible. You can stand clean and spotless before Him. Guilt will be gone, and you can be at peace. Go to your bishop. He holds the key to this cleansing power." (Conference Report, April 1972, p. 138.)

Many young people are concerned because the bishop also happens to be dad, or uncle, cousin, grandpa, or a close family friend. They know that having a relative for a bishop can sometimes make things a little more awkward. Heavenly Father understands the sensitivity of such a situation. "If for some reason (and this would be a very rare situation) the young person cannot possibly go to the bishop, he or she should be advised to go to the stake president" (Vaughn J. Featherstone, *A Generation of Excellence*, pp. 97-98).

"But what if the bishop or the stake president tells my parents?" Please remember that men who serve in these important priesthood offices are under a sacred obligation to keep completely confidential what they hear during interviews. What you say will never be repeated to counselors, wives, or behind your back in any way. If it is important that forgiveness be asked of another person, your leader will always ask your permission before involving anyone else. "Oh, yeah?" some might say. "Well, I heard about one bishop who . . . " Regrettably, we have all heard horror stories. But keep in mind that *if* the stories are true (and that is a big *if* as tales get taller) such a bishop is definitely the exception and not the rule.

When should I confess? Beyond transgressions that are obviously between you and God alone, far too many are willing to offer clear-cut lists of just what needs to be talked about with the bishop and what doesn't. Be cautious, for all sin is wrong. Making a distinction between "bad" sins that we must talk to a bishop about and "okay" sins that we don't have to speak to the bishop about seems as ridiculous and inappropriate as making a distinction between "okay" and "bad" R-rated movies when President Ezra Taft Benson has stated clearly that we should not see any at all (see *Ensign*, May 1986, p. 45).

The best response I have ever heard as to when one should confess to the bishop was given by President Roger Mack, a stake president in California. He said, "Whenever you wonder whether you should or shouldn't, you should."

If a list is needed, I think the best one to refer to is the one given us by the First Presidency in the helpful booklet *For the Strength of Youth*. It is appropriate and important to talk with a bishop about any violation of the standards clearly outlined in that booklet (see Elder Russell M. Nelson, *Ensign*, August 1991, p. 11).

Where do I confess? Confession can take place in a regular periodical interview in the bishop's office. But there are a lot of drawbacks in waiting until then. I admire young people who take the initiative to make an appointment to see the bishop. I have actually been with young people and literally held their hands as they have had the personal courage to make phone calls—even long-distance calls—to their bishops and set up private times and places to talk.

Why do I confess? Does God need us to outline each detail of our sins because he was taking a little nap during the last party we attended? No. After Adam and Eve partook of the forbidden fruit God asked them questions: Where goest thou? Who told thee thou wast naked? What is this thing which thou has done? (Moses 4:15-19.) Did God really need answers to such questions? Did he want responses for his sake or, like a wise and masterful teacher, did he want the questions answered for the sake of Adam and of Eve? Heavenly Father does not need knowledge or enlightenment. His children do. God does not need our confession as much as we need to confess.

"But it's scary," young people tell me again and again. It can be a little frightening when we finally face our deepest weaknesses and most debased actions. After their transgression even the noble Adam and Eve were afraid—they "went to hide themselves from the presence of the Lord God amongst the trees of the garden" (Moses 4:14). But could the trees hide them? Could their fig-leaf aprons (see Moses 4:13)? No more than our silence, avoidance, and procrastination can conceal our deeds and thoughts from God's all-seeing eyes.

However frightening confession may be, it is done for the sake of the transgressor, and it gives him the chance to do three important things: receive forgiveness from the Church; covenant to change; and receive help, counsel, and guidance in making the change.

Receive forgiveness from the Church. Elder Bruce R. McConkie wrote, "Ultimate forgiveness in all instances and for all sins comes from the Lord and from the Lord only." But, "the bishop is empowered to forgive sins as far as the Church is concerned." (*A New Witness for the Articles of Faith* [Salt Lake City: Deseret Book, 1985], p. 236.)

If a young man promises to take a girl to the prom and says he'll pick her up at six o'clock and then doesn't show up at all, he will have a deeply offended date, to say the least. He broke a promise. In this instance, would it be enough for him to only pray to Heavenly Father and ask forgiveness, or to talk to the bishop? Not really. In this case, God would expect him to seek the forgiveness of the young lady he had offended.

When we are baptized into the Church we witness before the Church that we have truly repented (see D&C 20:37). We make sacred covenants that we promise to keep always. Each Sabbath, as we take the sacrament, we renew those covenants. For Church members, a sin is not simply an offense against God but also is the breaking of a promise made to the Church. We must seek forgiveness from the church we have offended as well as from the Lord.

Covenant to change. Confession allows us to make new promises that we will adjust out lives. Ritualistically reporting details of sin without covenanting to change is as pointless as a cooking fire that gives no heat. Elder Orson Pratt wrote: "Confession should be accompanied with a promise and determination to sin no more. . . . Without a covenant or promise before God, that we will forsake sin with an unshaken determination that we will henceforth yield to no evil, our confession and repentance will be vain." ("True Repentance," in *A Series of Pamphlets by Orson Pratt,* pp. 31-32.)

Stephen R. Covey reminds us that willpower alone is not sufficient to make desired changes in character and that even sincere commitments will falter under pressure. Only in making covenants—two-way promises between man and God—can we tap the divine power source which can change our very natures and let us reach our potential. (See *The Divine Center* [Salt Lake City: Bookcraft, 1982], pp. 208, 221.)

Receive help, counsel, and guidance in making the change. Telling our sins to roommates, friends, or even family members may prove to be a temporary lifting of a heavy burden, but this feeling does not last. Even well-meant advice is just that—advice. The bishop, as the father of the ward, is the one who is authorized to receive inspiration in our behalf. He can offer us not just friendly advice but true help, counsel, and guidance. He can assist us in creating a positive plan of action that will let us grow, progress, break bad habits, and leave the past behind.

Sometimes, in extreme cases, the help the bishop offers will come in the form of an informal or formal probation, disfellowshipment, or even, in the most extreme cases, excommunication. All such actions entail a postponement of certain privileges of Church membership to one degree or other. At first glance, one might wonder how a probation or disfellowshipment can be considered helpful. We must realize that tough love is still love, and help, though considered hard at first, is still help. Wise students know that it is not always the easy teacher—the one who doesn't give homework or require the student's best efforts—who makes a difference.

How do I confess? In scriptures we are told to confess with godly sorrow (see 2 Corinthians 7:9-10), humility (see 2 Nephi 2:7; Alma 42:29-30), and completeness (see Leviticus 16:21).

Godly sorrow. President Ezra Taft Benson has written that real repentance requires a "deep, burning, and heartfelt sorrow for sin." This produces "a reformation of life. It is not just a confession of guilt." (*God, Family, Country* [Salt Lake City: Deseret Book, 1974], p. 196.)

I know one young woman who shoplifts. She feels sincerely sorry, regrets the unhappy consequences that have followed her choices, and feels guilt and remorse. But since she is doing nothing to come closer to Christ, her feelings are obviously superficial. I was at a stake dance where some young men showed up drunk. When they were confronted by their leaders and asked to leave, they felt sorry. But unless it helps them to change and do better, they only feel the kind of sorrow that, in more extreme circumstances, Mormon described as the "sorrowing of the damned" for "their sorrowing was not unto repentance" (see Mormon 2:12-14). Godly sorrow is that which leads to true repentance—a change in mind, motive, and manner.

Humility. King Benjamin describes a Judgment Day scene in

which the wicked have "an awful view of their guilt and abomina-
tions, which doth cause them to shrink from the presence of the
Lord" (Mosiah 3:25). But even those who have sinned grievously
can through mortal repentance change that scene to one of joy.
These repentant ones are truly humble. They are not justifying or
rationalizing their sins. They are not blaming others or making
weak excuses for their behavior. Those who are humble care little
about possible embarrassment, restrictions, or inconvenience
when they talk to the bishop. Their tears are real—not for show.
Their discouragement is sincere—not manipulative. Their words
are spontaneous—not pre-planned or rehearsed.

At one youth conference a young man pulled me aside and
asked to talk to me alone. With head held high and a cocky smile
on his face he proceeded to tell me about his immoral actions
with his nonmember girlfriend. This young man was shocked
when I said, "You sound more like you're bragging than confess-
ing." I contrast that young man's attitude with that of another
Aaronic Priesthood holder who found the courage to tell me that
he once had drunk a beer. He was completely crushed and devastated. As always, I encouraged him to talk to his bishop. He
thought about it for a long time. Finally, he said seriously, "Okay,
and I won't even care when he tells the ward."

"What?" I said in a surprised tone.

"Doesn't he have to tell the ward so they can vote on whether
I can still be a member of the Church?"

I would have laughed out loud, except that this young man
was so sincere. I explained his misunderstanding, assured him
that what he would tell his bishop would be kept confidential,
and expressed my admiration for his humility. "God resisteth the
proud, but giveth grace unto the humble" (James 4:6).

Completeness. I once received a letter asking: "When a person
repents for an action, does it include all the other times that it
has happened? What if a person who has confessed realizes that
he left out a minor detail? How far back in my past should I reach
when I confess and repent?" The answers to these questions are
obvious. "Do ye imagine to yourselves that ye can lie unto the
Lord?" (Alma 5:17.) Telling only some of our sins, our most recent
or socially acceptable sins, or disguising the seriousness or fre-
quency of our problems does little good.

One young man came to me and said: "I have done everything

I should. I've even talked to the bishop, but I still don't feel the peace, joy, and Spirit that I'm supposed to. What's wrong?"

"Perhaps," I suggested gently, "you didn't tell the bishop the whole story. Maybe he only got chapter one and part of chapter two. Do you still need to share the end of the book with him?" We went together and set another appointment—for him to tell the bishop—the rest of the story.

It is important to know the who, when, where, why and how of confession. But even more important is to remember that confession is only a means to an end—a part of the process of repentance. President Spencer W. Kimball wrote: "Confession brings peace. How often have people departed from my office relieved and lighter of heart than for a long time! Their burdens were lighter, having been shared. They were free. The truth had made them free." He explained that now these people felt "satisfaction in having taken another step in doing all that is possible to rid oneself of the burden of transgression." (*The Miracle of Forgiveness* [Salt Lake City: Bookcraft, 1969], pp. 187-88.)

In Doctrine and Covenants 58:43 we are told, "By this ye may know if a man repenteth of his sins—behold, he will confess them and forsake them." As important as confession is, the true test of repentance is in the forsaking of sin. President Ezra Taft Benson has stated: "Sometimes we regard all too lightly the principle of repentance, thinking that it only means confession, that it only means feeling sorry for ourselves. But it is more than that. It is . . . a deep, heartfelt sorrow for sin that produces a reformation of life. That is the right test: a reformation of life. Only then may the God of Heaven in his mercy and his goodness see fit to forgive us." (*God, Family, Country*, p. 196.)

In the Garden of Eden, after Adam and Eve confessed and made promises to change, they were given a garment to cover their nakedness. "Unto Adam, and also unto his wife, did I, the Lord God, make coats of skins, and clothed them" (Moses 4:27). As we confess—exposing our honest actions and innermost selves—and make positive changes, God will do for us what he did for Adam and Eve. In confession we bare our souls, uncover our past, and strip ourselves of pride. In that moment when feelings of imperfection, inadequacy, and shame are most intense—when we have, as it were, a "perfect knowledge of all our guilt and our uncleanness, and our nakedness"—God will clothe us. He will attire us in peace, joy, and forgiveness, just as he will ultimately array us in "robes of righteousness" (2 Nephi 9:14) and "garments of salvation" (Isaiah 61:10). He will redress us with his Spirit. In Christ's atonement we are, most literally, covered.

I'm sure my young friend who broke his arm when he was smashed by a falling human pyramid had not expected such an in-depth discussion. But while his broken bone left him unable to use his arm, his broken heart left him very able to use his conscience.

When we were finished at the hospital, I escorted my friend, complete with his new white cast, to the car. I said, "It's been a long night for you—in more ways than one." He nodded in agreement. "I challenge you to go see your bishop," I continued. "He works for God, and you can't get a better physician than that." We hugged—carefully—and I drove him home.

Not long afterwards a letter came: "Dear Brad: How are you? Myself? I am great, fantastic, stupendous, and better and cleaner than I have been since my baptism and it feels sooooo good. I saw my bishop and it was not as bad as I thought it would be. He told me he was glad that I made this decision in my life and that my life would run smoother now. . . . I asked him when I would be forgiven and he assured me that I would know. This week I lived my week normally, riding my bike every day and just hanging around with my friends, but today . . . I was in my room, listening to some Church music and the Spirit told me I was forgiven and that Jesus really loves me and knows me. It happened so fast that I did not know what was happening until I realized I was bawling like a baby. This is exactly what you said would happen . . . and it is one of the best things that has ever happened to me."

Brad Wilcox, a teacher on the Elementary Education faculty at BYU, spent his childhood years in Ethiopia and has traveled all over the world. He enjoys writing Church magazine articles, reading his kids bedtime stories, journal writing, and watching videos of classic movies. Two favorite former assignments are sixth-grade teacher and Primary chorister. Brad and his wife, Debi, have three children.

CHAPTER 9

"Beauty for Ashes": The Art of Seeing Miracles

Paula Thomas

I believe in miracles! I believe that clouds do have silver linings and that it is always darkest just before the dawn. I believe in guardian angels; in a loving Father in Heaven; and that life is a test that we need to experience and grow from. We pass this test not just by having all the right answers or the best experiences that this life has to offer, but by doing the best we can with the circumstances we've been given and with the choices (be they good or not so good) that we make while on this earth.

I once asked a group of sixteen- and seventeen-year-old young women what excited them about their lives; what lit them at this moment in time. They had difficulty in answering the question. Several girls even asked if they could tell me what depressed them or caused them to be down. Many of them agreed that that would be a far easier question to answer than the question, "What lights your life?" I pondered this experience for weeks after—realizing how many times in my life I have not been able to see the light but have instead chosen to see the dark or down side of my circumstance or experience.

One afternoon while preparing to teach a lesson I ran across a scripture in Isaiah (Isaiah 61:3) that caused my mind to flood with thoughts on how well Heavenly Father knows his children (you and me). He knew that our human nature could easily fall to the negative side of our earthly experiences, and he told us that in this verse. Isaiah was prophesying about the coming of the Messiah and what his coming would mean to us as his children. The Messiah would come "to give unto them beauty for ashes, the oil of joy for mourning, the garment of praise for the spirit of heaviness; that they might be called trees of righteousness [children of God]."

Along with Christ's coming to atone for our sins, he would show us by his example that our freedom of choice, or agency, is not just the right to choose between good and evil but also the right to choose every minute of every day how we will respond to life's experiences and to the people who share those experiences with us. The life of Jesus was a constant example of choosing the higher ground.

How do your eyes see your world? Do you see the not-so-nice clothes, or the goodness of the person wearing the clothes? Do you see the flower, or the weed that grows next to it? Do you count your blessings, or your flaws? Do you see the beauty, or do you see the ashes? What are your ashes, or the difficulties in your life that you need to rise above?

As for me, one of my great challenges as I entered my teen years was the house I lived in. It had always been fine, as houses go, when I was just a kid, but being in eighth grade had kind of changed things. I lived in a rural area of South Salt Lake, and I always felt for the most part that I fit in okay. Then I passed the sixth grade and moved on to the big-time junior high school. Several elementary schools fed into this school. There seemed to be so many people; how would I ever get to know them?

Seventh grade was rough, but I made it. In the last part of that year I was beginning to make friends and finally feel a part of the crowd. But I began to notice what I perceived to be a big difference between my friends and myself, and that was the houses we lived in. Their homes seemed to me to be palaces. They were brick—they had carpet and nice bathrooms. Beautiful furniture was all around, and the kitchens had all of the modern appliances.

Choosing to see the "ashes," I saw that my home was small, it was ugly on the outside, and it was a basement. That meant that it was kind of underground; it was a basement without the upstairs built on yet. Surely if my friends saw where I lived I would no longer have any friends. I was often asked why we couldn't come to my house to sleep over or just to watch TV, but I was always ready with a great excuse. I knew it was only a matter of time before they found out. What could I do to make my house look better? The idea finally came! I would paint my front door.

Let me explain my reasoning. My house was only three to four feet above the ground, and the weeds around it (we were in the middle of a field) were about that high. It had a flat roof that you could walk on (although you weren't supposed to) and a door; one door that stood on the top of the roof at the east end of the house. The door was the only part of the house that really showed at all. It was weather-beaten and worn. I thought that if my door looked better, maybe it would make the whole house look better.

With baby-sitting money I purchased paint, sandpaper, and a paint brush. Color was difficult. I finally decided on green, to match nature; don't ask me why! I went to work. I sanded it until it was as smooth as glass—then I began to paint. High gloss, oil-base enamel; one coat right after the other until the small can of paint had been wiped clean. The color looked quite bright to me, but it was still wet—that had to be the reason.

The next morning I went out to look at my new door. I stood as far back on the porch as I could without falling off, and it still looked really bright. I touched the door to see if it was dry. It was dry. It was bright. It was so bright that it seemed to glow from inside. I went down to the garbage can and retrieved the paint container. I had not noticed one important word on the can—*fluorescent*. I had painted my door with fluorescent green paint! It glowed in the sunlight for miles around.

My bus stop was a mile and a quarter from my house. As the bus would come to a stop, people who had never noticed my house before would now ask, "What's that green door doing standing in the middle of that field?" What was really great was how my door looked on nights when there was a full moon. It was like a neon sign advertising, "Paula lives here, Paula lives here." There was a popular song at the time on the radio called "What's Behind the Green Door?" I was asked that question a lot! It took me several years to live down my "green door."

There was much that was beautiful about my house. The inside was spotlessly clean and always smelled of homemade goodies. Surrounded by giant cottonwood trees, it was always cool and quiet in the summertime. When I would go away for even a night, I was always anxious to come home. I wish now that I could have made a better choice; I wish I had seen the beauty.

The next gift that the Messiah will bring is the "oil of joy for mourning." How does this apply to you and me? There are different levels of mourning. Many of us have lost a loved one who suffered from a disease or encountered a fatal accident. Others of us have suffered or mourned over problems that seemed at the time to have no solution—we have felt despair. I believe that in these most painful hours come our sweetest experiences with a Father in Heaven who is aware of our pain.

Years ago my husband and I loaded up our old green Ford station wagon with a cooler full of food and our four small children and headed for Grand Junction, Colorado. It was a joyful occasion because our sweetest friends had just been baptized members of the Church. We were there to celebrate. After we had rejoiced with them for a couple of days, it was time for us to head home. Because of our financial situation at the time, we referred to trips such as this one as "wing and prayer" trips. We never had quite enough money to make any trip feel too safe.

On this occasion we put our last ten dollars into our gas tank and headed for home. We were about midway between Grand Junction and Salt Lake City on a desolate stretch of freeway when our green station wagon began making a very interesting noise and black smoke started working its way out from under the hood. My husband pulled out of the traffic lane onto the emergency strip. I saw on his face total fear and desperation, because he was not a mechanic. If something was wrong with our car we were going to be very stranded.

There was very little traffic on the freeway that afternoon, so we backed the car up to an exit sign a few yards back from where we had stopped. Along with the exit sign was a sign that read "Services." The word had been crossed out. We followed the exit road down to an old gas station that was all boarded up. My husband turned the engine off, and we all sat in silence.

Our children, even though they were very young, were intuitively aware of the anxiety that hovered in the car. My husband, Dave, got out of the car and looked under the hood, hoping that something would leap to his attention that he would be able to fix with his limited knowledge of mechanics. He saw nothing but left-over black smoke. We were in trouble. Our hearts were heavy with the desperation of the moment. As parents we were mourning the circumstances we had placed our little family in by undertaking a "wing and prayer" adventure.

As we all sat in silence, a little voice from the back of the car said, "Dad, can't you give our car a blessing and make it better, just like you do with people?" We turned to look at our six-year-old son, Jim. His eyes were full of confidence that his suggestion would work. It was as if he couldn't figure out why we hadn't thought of it.

A very teachable father followed the counsel of an inspired six-year-old and said, "I think first we all need to pray together; then I will go out and bless our car." We offered a prayer, then Dave went out to the front of the car. He shut the hood and gently placed his hands on our only way home. Four little sets of eyes looked on without a doubt in their minds that, with the priesthood, Dad was going to heal their green station wagon. Dave gave the car a sweet and gentle blessing, then returned to the driver's seat to turn on the ignition.

As the engine started we waited to see if the black smoke was still our companion. No smoke came. We returned to the freeway to finish off the last leg of our adventure.

We felt so lost and alone as we sat in front of that skeleton of a station, but in the darkest of moments came a loving Father in Heaven to offer us the "oil of joy," to show us his hand in our lives—to heal even a car.

We had been home for two days when the black smoke and the noise came again. We had, as mechanics would say, thrown a rod. The repair was so big that the car was not worth fixing.

I know there are people in this world who would say that this experience was just plain luck; or maybe that the car was not in that bad a shape. Some of you might say that kind of thing never happens to you. Maybe you feel that you have never had a prayer answered, or you think you've never had a spiritual experience. Isaiah was saying to you and me that we need to open our eyes a little wider, rely a little more on our spirit, listen a little more intently to the still, small voice within us so that we can see God's hand in our lives—so we can see the light. I feel that if God knows that we are watching more carefully and listening a little harder, he will give us moments of enlightenment that reveal the miracles in simple things.

In 1984 we took our six children to Disneyland (this was not a "wing and prayer" trip). Our youngest son, Jon, was almost four years old. He had only one purpose on this journey, and that was to see Winnie the Pooh. The real live Winnie the Pooh. His little mind could not grasp the concept of *cartoon,* and we were concerned that he would be disappointed.

Our day in Disneyland was wonderful, but we could not find Winnie the Pooh. As the sun was setting, however, and we were walking down Main Street, there surrounded by children was the big yellow bear. Jon was the first one to spot him. The bear was in the middle of the street and Jon was on the sidewalk. Jon's eyes focused on nothing else but the person wearing the costume of Winnie the Pooh.

We all stopped to see what would happen with this little four-year-old. The young man in the bear suit spotted my son standing apart from us on the sidewalk in a trance. He let the other children know that he would be right back. That six-foot-tall yellow bear walked over to Jon, bent down, and touched his big black nose to Jon's nose. "Winnie the Pooh kissed me!" squealed a totally delighted four-year-old.

This story brings to my mind two important points. First, how simple this experience was. Winnie the Pooh had been a topic of conversation in our home every time we talked about or made plans for this trip to Disneyland. Our experience on Main Street that evening was so significant to us all because we loved Jon and we were concerned and curious as to how he would respond to people in costumes instead of "real" characters. It was a simple concern that mattered to no one else but us. It wasn't Mickey Mouse or Donald Duck or Goofy that stood in the middle of the street as the sun was setting—it was Winnie the Pooh. This bear singled out Jon, even though he was surrounded by sixteen to twenty other children, and walked right over to the sidewalk where our little son was standing. This said to the minds of each member of our family that someone else had heard our conversations and knew our concerns (as simple as they were) and wanted us to know that we had been heard and he was aware.

Have you ever been thinking about a friend—and he calls? You might respond to that by thinking how "weird" that was. Have you ever listened to a speaker or a teacher and when she was through you just had to tell her that she had said just what you wanted or needed to hear? In your prayers you had even talked about this exact information. Have you ever felt totally alone—and there came a knock at the door? Heavenly Father is showing us all the time, in simple but meaningful ways, that he is aware of us and our concerns. We tend to describe the experiences with the wrong words: "It was so weird that that happened." "Boy, was I ever lucky!" "Talk about a coincidence!" "What a small world!"

The second point the Disneyland experience makes is how God can and does use us for good in the lives of other people. This point brings me to the final section of this article: "the garment of praise for the spirit of heaviness." We can all have the opportunity of being angels in the lives of others. We also have the capacity of being "little black rain clouds," as Winnie the Pooh sings so well. In order to replace heaviness or sadness and despair with light, or praise, or thoughtfulness and love, we have to learn to tune in to others and be aware of them. That means we have to give away some of ourselves; maybe not think so much of the time about what we need or want but open our eyes to see what we could do for someone else. When we discover what we could do to lighten someone else's load we should not walk but run to accomplish our mission. The man in the bear costume at Disneyland felt prompted to approach a little blond-haired, blue-eyed boy and make him feel important. Because he listened, he became a large part of a little miracle. The choice is up to us. How do you choose?

As for me, I believe in miracles. I believe in a loving Father in Heaven who is involved in our lives and who wants us to know of his involvement. I testify to the reality of this truth.

Paula Thomas is a Laurel advisor in Sandy, Utah. She is currently working on a degree in Family Science at Brigham Young University and enjoys reading, writing, and caring for her family and home. She loves working with youth and has served as a Young Women president. She and her husband, David (who also authored a chapter for this book), are the parents of six children.

CHAPTER 10

The Search for Intensity

Todd Parker

Why do people stand in line for three hours for a ninety-second ride on the "Viper" at Six Flags Magic Mountain Amusement Park in California? Why do young people love loud rock music, skydiving, hang gliding, bungi-cord jumping, water skiing, or snow skiing? Why do they love dances, racing motorcycles, and shooting the rapids? Why do people pay unbelievable prices to see Olympic competition? Why do they watch soap operas or play video games? Why did 90,000 Romans fill the Colosseum to watch the gladiators and 250,000 fill Circus Maximus to see a chariot race? Why do people take drugs, fall into immorality, watch R- and X-rated movies or horror movies, read pornography, or shoplift (even though they may have plenty of money)?

The answer to all of these questions is one common element—these people are seeking *intensity*. Some may call it excitement or use the terms *rush*, *high*, *buzz*, *kicks*, or *thrills*. Whatever it is called, most people, especially young people, seek intensity. They want an exhilarating, heart-pounding, emotionally charged experience. Some people look for it through appropriate means, while others seek their intensity inappropriately.

Intensity comes in different forms and can be provided in different ways. Competition in the areas of sports, popularity, or academics provides a measure of intensity. A goodnight scene on the porch, where the boy is thinking, "so help me, I'll kiss you," and the girl is thinking, "so kiss me, I'll help you!" can be intense. A football game with ten seconds to play and your team behind by five points on the opposing team's eight-yard line can be intense.

Other people seek their intensity through music, music videos, or concerts. Michael Jackson's video, "Thriller," broke sales records because people liked the intense experience it provided.

There is a common feeling among some of today's youth that the only way to have fun or feel some intensity is through wrongdoing. The purpose of this chapter is not only to outline a few ways in which youth can understand a little better this desire we all share for intensity, but also to outline a few principles and ideas that may help youth find through appropriate activities the intensity they are seeking. You do not have to sin to feel this intensity. You can find it through ways that are in harmony with the gospel. What follows is a list of four areas wherein youth can experience intensity or excitement without sinning or compromising their standards.

1. *Missionary work is exciting.* Too often young men feel that they don't want to serve a full-time mission because it will be boring. I'll admit that I entered the mission field thinking, "The next two years will be all hard, serious, spiritual, intensity-lacking experiences." I was blessed with a companion who taught me otherwise. He said, "Everything we do is exciting. It all depends on your attitude." He said, "We need to set goals. The more people we see, the more we'll baptize." We bought counters and kept them in our pockets. We set goals of how many people we'd see before lunch or by dinner time. It got exciting. Instead of saying, "Man, it's eleven-thirty; let's go in a little early for lunch" we would look at our pocket counters and say, "We need to see thirty-seven more people before we quit for lunch!" We would actually run down the street, hurdling fences and jumping hedges. One morning in Culver City, California, we set up seventeen first discussions. One of those led to a second, a third, and so on, and we baptized a wonderful lady. It was a great experience.

Can you imagine the intensity felt by the former missionary in the following story told by Elder Harold B. Lee?

"I remember the story that Brother Charles A. Callis used to tell us. There was a missionary who went over to Ireland and had filled a mission of two or three years. They invited him to the stand to give his homecoming speech, and he said to them something like this: 'Brothers and sisters, I think my mission has been a failure. I have labored all my days as a missionary here and I have only baptized one dirty little Irish kid. That is all I baptized.'

"Years later this man came back, went up to his home somewhere in Montana, and Brother Callis, now a member of the Council of the Twelve, learned where he was living, this old missionary, and went to visit him. And he said to him, 'Do you remember having served as a missionary over in Ireland? And do you remember having said that you thought your mission was a failure because you only baptized one dirty little Irish kid?'

"He said, 'Yes.'

"Well, Brother Callis put out his hand, and he said: 'I would like to shake hands with you. My name is Charles A. Callis, of the Council of the Twelve of The Church of Jesus Christ of Latter-day Saints. I am that dirty little Irish kid that you baptized on your mission.'" (Harold B. Lee, *Feet Shod with the Preparation of the Gospel of Peace*, *Speeches of the Year*, 9 November 1954, p. 1.)

For any young man who is deliberating whether or not he would like to fill a mission, allow me to share the words of a modern apostle, Elder George G. Richards.

"In the name of the Lord I want to promise you that in the acceptance of the mission call and the dedication of yourself to the work, the Lord will forgive you of past transgressions, and you can start out life with an absolutely clean sheet" (quoted by Elder Carlos E. Asay, *Ensign*, October 1985, p. 52).

What a wonderful promise! If you accept the call and dedicate yourself to the work, when you step off the plane that brings you home you are spotless—your slate is wiped clean!

2. *Anticipation creates intensity.* Anticipating an event or looking forward to something can provide excitement. Proverbs 29:18 states, "Where there is no vision, the people perish." We all need something to look forward to.

I read somewhere that the best part of a kiss is not when the lips meet: that, rather, the moment of anticipation immediately before the two pairs of lips come together is when the excitement is at its peak. I tell my female students that if that is the truth, then when a boy brings a girl home from a date the girl should let him lean over and get within about one-half inch of her lips and then say, "That was great!" Then she should go into the house, because they have experienced the anticipation, which is the best part of the kiss!

Another way of viewing anticipation is goal setting. Once goals are in place we find excitement in our progression toward reaching that goal. Absence of goals or of anticipation often causes depression and despair. An illustration of this principle comes to us in the form of a story about a boy who lived in Shelley, Idaho.

One day while irrigating on a farm, this young man climbed a power pole to see where his friends were. His knee inadvertently touched a twelve-thousand-volt line. The shock knocked him from the pole, and he fell twenty-five feet. His heart had been stopped by the electricity, but the impact of his body hitting the ground started it again. He screamed, and his friends came running. His knees had been "blown away." There was very little flesh left on his legs.

He was rushed to the hospital, but the doctors gave his family little hope that he would live. They shot him full of morphine for his pain and waited. When morning came and he was still alive, they amputated both of his legs twelve inches below his hips.

Prior to the accident he had stood six feet seven inches tall and weighed 195 pounds. When he finally left the hospital in a wheelchair he weighed 73 pounds, and was struggling to get off morphine.

In such circumstances, what would you do? Would you give up? feel sorry for yourself? Not Curt Brinkman. Who would have guessed that ten years later he would win the Boston Marathon in a wheelchair? He covered that 26-mile, 385-yard course in one hour and fifty-five minutes. He beat Bill Rogers, the first-place able-bodied runner, by seventeen minutes and broke the wheelchair record by twenty-nine minutes! There's something else— Curt Brinkman is diabetic. To keep his blood sugar level normal, he has to carry bottles of orange juice to sip when he races.

He is one of the greatest champions that ever lived! How did he do it? He set goals, and the anticipation of reaching those goals provided a needed intensity with which to overcome the depression and despair that gripped him when he came home from the hospital that first day.

If you are down or depressed and life seems to hold little

meaning, do as Curt Brinkman did. Set goals. Look to the future and work on the goals a little at a time. As you make progress you'll find that you feel an excitement and intensity return to your life.

3. *Avoid seeking intensity from a wrong source.* Be careful of the music of the world. Many young people seek their intensity in certain types of rock music. The Brethren have counseled us to be careful about this.

Elder Gene R. Cook told of an experience he had on an airplane with one of the world's most famous rock stars. Elder Cook didn't recognize him at first, but the singer pointed to a picture of himself in a rock magazine and said, "That's me."

Elder Cook then asked him a question. He said: "Some of the young people I'm with tell me that rock music, the kind that you and others are involved with, has no real impact on them—for good or for evil. You've been in this thing for twenty years. What is your opinion?"

The rock star replied, "Our music is calculated to drive the kids to sex." He saw Elder Cook's startled reaction and then added: "Of course, it's up to them what they do. It's not my fault. I'm just making a lot of money."

The conversation continued. The rock singer said that he was delighted that the family was being destroyed around the world. Elder Cook told him that he had eight children. The singer said that he had children, too, but no wife. He said that he had made a woman pregnant in Virginia, another in New York, and another in England.

He then told Elder Cook that he had had the missionary lessons and said, "Anyone who believes the Book of Mormon to be the word of God is a liar, and the Book of Mormon is a lie."

Elder Cook replied by saying: "You are very fortunate today, because you are sitting next to a servant of the Lord who is going to correct what you just said." He placed a Book of Mormon on the man's lap and said: "I have read this book many times and believe it to be the word of God. You show me one chapter that is a lie." (The rock star was silent.) "You show me one page. How about one paragraph? How about one line? How about one word?" Then Elder Cook said to the singer, "I bear testimony that you are the liar and the Book of Mormon is the word of God." He then warned the singer that the Lord would hold him responsible to the degree that he understood what Elder Cook was saying.

(From address given at Ricks College Devotional, November 29, 1988.)

The Lord's way to feel intensity is through his Spirit and his gospel. Satan's counterfeit is often music, sex, or drugs. When the people producing the music admit their motives and those motives are in that category of Satan's counterfeits, we would do well to stay as far away from those influences as we possibly can.

4. *Intense experiences can occur as we "obey the voice of the Spirit" (1 Nephi 4:18).*

An example of this was printed in the *Salt Lake Deseret News* on August 6, 1934. A man named Cook was plowing his field near Tremonton, Utah, back in 1916. His three little boys were riding on the tractor behind him. Suddenly he noticed that two of the boys were running out in front of the tractor waving their arms. He looked back to see that the rear wheel of that huge tractor had just run over and crushed his five-year-old son. Immediately he stopped that tractor, scooped the boy up, and began to run for the house. He said that just as he passed the tractor the Spirit told him to kneel down. He did so, holding the boy's flattened head in his hands. Afterwards he said, "With intelligence not my own, I brought the head back into shape," and he repeated words of administration while holding the boy's head in his hands.

The doctor said the injury was a complete diagonal skull fracture from the top of his right eye to the back of his left ear. He said that only one in a hundred would ever recover from such an injury, but this boy completely recovered. The boy went on to receive a master's degree in chemistry from the University of Utah and was chosen one of sixty to enter the Yale University Chemical Department. He became a respected scientist and authored the book, *Science and Mormonism*.

The Spirit of God and the power of his priesthood provide a real intensity which is good. It is one which involves light and truth and will not deceive you. Satan's counterfeits provide sin, deception, and darkness. The lasting intensity which the Holy Ghost brings, with its attendant warmth, love, and joy, are in sharp contrast to Satan's quick counterfeit intensity that leaves you empty, void of the Spirit, and spiritually bankrupt. When a person falls into the temptation of partaking of momentary pleasures, he is at odds with himself. He feels anxious inside, guilty, despairing, and has an insatiable desire for his next thrill. When a person bases his life on feeling the constant companionship of the Holy Ghost, the intensity he finds is not shallow or hollow but warm, glowing, and fulfilling. It motivates him to do good and serve others.

I hope that we can each realize that although finding intensity through good and appropriate ways may be harder and may take longer than succumbing to Satan's quick counterfeits, the Lord's rewards are abundant, sure, and lasting; and their consequences, unlike those of following the adversary, will always be positive and uplifting. May we all seek and find our intensity in the Lord's way.

Todd Parker, an institute instructor in Tucson, Arizona, holds a doctorate in Educational Psychology from Brigham Young University. Todd likes pole vaulting (he once held the state record in Utah for the pole vault), distance running, gymnastics, and snow and water skiing (he also set an AUU record in cross-country running). He enjoys the energy and enthusiasm of youth and finds that young people "are never boring." Todd and his wife, Debbie, have seven children.

CHAPTER 11

Finding the Light of the Lord in Deep Waters and Dark Times

A. David Thomas

I am afraid of snakes, and I have been afraid of the dark. I've felt fear, even terror, at the thought of speaking in front of people and being judged or evaluated by others. I've been a worrier all my life, and I have a vivid imagination. I've spent more than my fair share of time in the dark and in deep water. I think I'm an expert on fear.

When the Lord, through the scriptures, speaks about fear, he identifies two kinds. The first is desirable. This kind of fear is called a "fear of the Lord." This fear implies a reverence, an awe, and a deep respect for God, his ways, commandments, and plan, and suggests that we should back away from anything that could risk, frustrate, or in any way imperil our ability to be with and on God's side. This fear is productive and proactive. This fear is sensible and justified. Paul called this fear "godly fear" (Hebrews 12:28).

A second kind of fear that is identified in the scriptures seems to stupefy and stall righteous action. The Lord and his prophets would have us avoid this destructive fear. Unproductive fear can be cast out with love (see Moroni 8:16), righteousness (see D&C 6:33-34), and preparation (see D&C 38:30). Our Heavenly Father would have us push through fears that cause doubts and hesitations, because they remove the blessings that come from faith-filled action: "Ye endeavored to believe that ye should receive the blessing which was offered unto you; but . . . there were fears in your hearts, and . . . this is the reason that ye did not receive" (D&C 67:3).

But a careful reading of the scriptures reveals that, with the possible exception of Jesus, many if not all of the "noble and great ones" have at some time suffered from unproductive fear. Gideon needed some sheepskin miracles to overcome his fears and become the Lord's "mighty man of valor" (see Judges 6:12, 36-40). Jacob's fear of the revenge of his brother, Esau, caused him to take elaborate precautions and seek to placate Esau with gifts (see Genesis 32:6-20). Even the young Joseph Smith "was ready to sink into despair and abandon [himself] to destruction" (Joseph Smith—History 1:16). It would appear that there is an interaction or conflict between righteous and unproductive fears, and that this conflict is the appropriate lot of those who have come to earth to fulfill our Heavenly Father's plan.

The prophet Moses provides a good example of the interaction of the two fears. The Old Testament tells us that Moses was the meekest of men (see Numbers 12:3). We think of *meek* as meaning being teachable, submissive, and patient, all worthy attributes. But the Moses we meet in Exodus chapter 4 sounds afraid of the assignment. Moses began to make excuses to the Lord, suggesting reasons why he was the wrong man for the job.

The Lord called him to be His spokesman, and Moses replied, "They will not believe me nor hearken unto my voice." But the Lord assured him that they would, and he provided Moses with some signs or miracles to convince the unbelievers. The Lord taught him how to turn his staff into a snake and back into a staff. He also provided a leprous-hand miracle that I'm sure impressed Moses, because it was Moses' hand that the Lord turned white with the disease and then healed. Then the Lord showed Moses how to change water into blood. But in spite of the Lord's effort to persuade, Moses held his ground. He said, "I am not eloquent . . . I am slow of speech and of a slow tongue."

The Lord tried again. He said, "I will be with thy mouth and teach thee what thou shalt say." But Moses pleaded with the Lord to send someone else. The scriptures indicate that the Lord now was angry with Moses because of his fears. He gave Moses his brother, Aaron, as a spokesman. The Lord said, "He shall be to thee instead of a mouth, and thou shalt be to him instead of God. . . . and [I] will teach you what ye shall do." (See Exodus 4:1-16.)

The important lesson here is that in spite of his fears, Moses went. He mastered those fears and threw his staff in at Pharaoh's feet, where as a serpent it swallowed the magicians' rod—serpents, while Aaron spoke boldly the words of God that came from Moses' lips. Ten times Moses fought for God against the power of Egypt and its Pharaoh, until the most arrogant of men bowed his will to the words of the meekest of men and the children of Israel were set free.

Prophets or ordinary sinners, we all have our fears. As I've told you, I have been afraid of the dark. I was the victim of a wonderful imagination. To my unenlightened mind the absence of light meant the presence of horrible things. I would quiver in the sheets of my bed and assume the walls were covered with spiders, the floor crawled with snakes and ghouls, and the air vibrated with demons, banshees, and ghosts, just waiting for me to let my guard down. Now, this was not the problem of a small child but rather a young man well on his way into high school, and my father, a sensitive man, realized I was distressed, because fifteen-year-olds normally don't want to sleep with their parents.

"What is it, son?" he asked from his bed.

"Nothing," I replied, but my eyes were wide with fear and my body was covered with sweat.

My dad pulled back the sheets and got up. He walked me into the living room. We sat down. "You're frightened, aren't you?" he said.

"Yes!"

"Of what?"

"I don't know."

These are the times when good fathers pass muster. "You know, son," my father started, "when I was your age, living in Varteg, Wales, I had to walk down the hill and get water out of a well for my mother. It seemed to me that your grandmother always wanted water in the middle of the night. I always tried to talk her out of it, but Mothers don't always listen to fifteen-year-old boys, and I would find myself out in the dark, afraid. In my mind, son, the night was filled with frightful things. In my mind, the worst of things lived in the dark. Somehow your grandfather sensed my fears, and one night he walked into the dark with me."

(I don't know why, but my father and I were sitting in the dark. We hadn't turned on the lights.)

"My dad, your grandpa, told me to look up at the sky, and we looked at it together. He told me of pictures in the sky, framed with stars. He reminded me of warm summer breezes and moonlight. We talked of winter nights, and stars dropping their light, and the new snow sparkling back the favor. He talked of the future, girls, love, and again of moonlight. He told me of rest, sleep, and beautiful dreams, all products of the nighttime. And he reminded me that a child, the Light of the world, came down to us in the dark, at nighttime. Your grandfather explained that fear of the dark or other things is the first test of growing up. To be full tall we must face our fears, push through, and see the beauty on the other side."

My dad and I walked outside. We looked at the stars, and then we both went to bed and slept well.

So much of unproductive fear is a matter of how you see it. My dad, as his dad had done, simply expanded my definition of the dark; and with a new view, with time, and with the moonlight my fear of the dark went away.

Life is full of these kinds of transitional fears, fears we have to face, interpret, and move through. All of us have to intersect and pass through our fears. Nephi had to resist his fear of change and allow the Lord to soften his heart so that he didn't rebel, as his older brothers did (see 1 Nephi 2:16). Adam and Eve accepted death in order that we might exist in mortality (see Moses 5:11). Esther risked her station as queen and also her life to plead for the lives of her people (see Esther 4:11, 14; 5:1-2). Noah, Lehi, the brother of Jared, and Joseph Smith each risked humiliation to warn a people and save their children. Hannah took risks, and covenanted with the Lord for a son; and when the Lord blessed her with one, she kept her promise and returned him to God, thus giving Israel the prophet Samuel (see 1 Samuel 1-3). And Abraham, living in a wicked world, looked past its ugliness and courageously sought the blessings of the fathers (see Abraham 1:1-4). Fear is always there just trying to get a hold on us. It can be both our nemesis and our friend. Fear can keep us from becoming ourselves, but it can also keep us from danger. How can we know the difference between righteous and nonproductive fear?

A friend of mine, Dr. Lynn Johnson, told me a disturbing story. It seems that in the northern parts of Wisconsin the lake water never really gets warm. The ice barely melts from the surface of the lakes before the winter snow begins to fall. As a result lake swimming is not big in those northern parts of Wisconsin, and in remote areas where there are no heated covered pools many people never learn to swim.

One day in late summer, in one of these cold-water areas, a group of teenagers was having a party on the edge of a lake. Part of the group was playing on a boat dock that reached far out into the lake, and as a result of a playful struggle one of the boys was knocked into the water. He screamed out in terror that he could not swim, and he fought frantically to keep on the top of the water. The other young people struggled to reach him, but he was beyond their reach and there wasn't a swimmer among them. The boy splashed desperately to reach for them as they in turn groped hopelessly for him. Finally, realizing their dilemma, two boys ran to get the park ranger. Running both ways they quickly returned with the ranger, but to their heartache they found their friend floating face down in the water.

It was then that something truly shocking happened. The ranger waded out into the water right up to the side of the corpse of the drowned boy. It was only waist deep. If the boy had only stood up he could have walked out of the lake, but in his fear he died helpless in a totally manageable situation.

The Lord would have us master our fears of just trying life out. We must all learn to swim in the struggles of just being alive and becoming ourselves. Doing is living. We mustn't be afraid of "having a go." Fear that keeps us from becoming and obeying is unproductive fear.

Florence Chadwick of California was a remarkable swimmer. She was the first woman to swim the English Channel from England to France, which she did in 16 hours and 19 minutes on 11 September 1953. Later she would swim that channel two other times. The total point-to-point distance was twenty-one miles, but allowing for cross-currents, experts placed the actual swimming distance at closer to fifty miles.

Florence was truly a remarkable swimmer, and that's what makes what happened on 4 July 1952 so strange. The swim was to Catalina Island, twenty-one miles off the coast of southern California. She started her swim using the deep hard strokes she had developed swimming off the coast of San Diego. The swim continued without a hitch until she was just a half mile from the

Catalina coast, at which point she raised up in the water to see how much further she had to go. The coast was shrouded in fog; she could not see her goal; and to the amazement of those rowing in her support boat she quit and climbed into the boat. Her support crew could hear the surf crashing against the Catalina coast, but Florence saw only fog; she couldn't see the coast, so she quit.

The devil loves this kind of fear-induced failure because the hero has already paid the price of conquest, but he or she leaves the field empty-handed and dejected. Discouragement is an ugly form of fear, and in a righteous cause it can be overcome with the aid of prayer, scripture study, service, and the support of friends.

While discouragement and doubt are ugly forms of unproductive fear, not all fear is bad. Some fear comes as a warning—a warning to back away, to quit. These fears warn that the risk is too high and not worth the cost. This is a fear we all need to recognize and heed. Such fears alert us that we are entering evil and forbidden waters.

On 25 August 1875, Captain Matthew Webb became the first human to swim the English Channel unassisted. This swim would make him famous; the press would acknowledge him as the world's greatest swimmer. Thousands flocked to see him swim using the stroke that conquered the channel. He gave demonstrations of his endurance. At one point he won four hundred English pounds for swimming more than seventy-four hours. Progressively he became more of a stuntman than an athlete, hence he yearned for another great swim. As his popularity waned in England he moved to the United States, where he and his manager continued to look for the "Big One." Captain Webb needed to make some real money. He had a wife and two children to support.

And then they found it—the elusive "Big One!" It was Niagara Falls. Below those falls lay a stretch of the angriest water on the face of the earth. If Webb could swim it his fame would be restored.

On a late summer day in 1883, the thirty-five-year-old, two-hundred-pound swimmer stood on the edge of the Niagara River just below the falls. At this point the river funnels into two steep walls, causing the speed of the water to accelerate to over thirty-five miles per hour. The surface of the water billows with angry waves, some reaching over twenty-five feet high. Then the river cascades into the whirlpool rapids, which continue for over a mile; and below these rapids the whirlpool itself gapes hungry for the stupid. Webb saw all of this. His only comment was, "It's a rum bit of water."

In spite of wiser counsel he got into a boat and was rowed out into the center of the river, where he jumped in and started swimming. Five hundred spectators watched this foolhardy enterprise. With powerful strokes Webb pulled towards the whirlpool rapids. Then he disappeared. The water just swallowed him. The swim lasted only four minutes, and the body was not found for four days. He had been caught by those furious waters, and he died in mid-stroke. The doctors who examined the body said that the force of the water had pressed the life right out of him. For a past-the-prime effort to recapture the "Big One," he left his wife and two children with no support. A wise sense of fear said "back off," but he didn't listen.

So some fears must be worked through, and others offer a whispered "Back away." How we interact with these fears determines the quality and scope of our life.

A proper response to a fear can leave us with a magnificent memory. A few years back I had a goal, a dream. I was going to Egypt, and I wanted to run in the morning desert sun from the Sphinx to the Pyramids of Giza. A short run, but it would be a memorable one. I held a vision in my heart and mind of me racing across the deserts of Cairo as the sun danced on the eternal steps of Cheops.

I arrived in Egypt at the height of Ramadan, a month-long period of fasting that all devout Muslims observe. From dawn to darkness each day of that month the faithful of Islam fast to purify their lives and thereby produce extra food and money for the poor. Cairo is unbelievable at Ramadan, especially at night. Colored lights hang everywhere, and the faithful fill the streets as at dark they rush to happily end their daily fast. As I watched that first night, the eager hungry pressed against each other and the side of the bus. The noise and the strangeness of this new world frightened me, and I was glad I sat safely with people I knew. My first night in Africa was a frightening one, especially for someone who had a history of being afraid—afraid of the dark and of the unknown.

Well, my days in Egypt passed quickly, and soon my last day turned from daylight to dark. I had not fulfilled my desert dream run. Outside, after days of my learning to understand and appreciate Muslim ways and Muslim people, the noise and dark of Ramadan waited along with the Sphinx and the Pyramids. I ran out into the dark. I ran past the happy Egyptians eating and rejoicing in their faith. I ran up to the ancient face of the Sphinx and said my good-byes, and then I turned and ran up the hill to the majesty of the Pyramids of Giza. Thus, with the lights of Cairo flickering behind me, I fulfilled a daylight dream in the dark I had once feared.

I pray that you will overcome your foolish fears and be responsive to all of your righteous ones.

A. David Thomas, who holds a Ph.D. in Education, teaches in seminary, in youth and family programs at BYU, and in business classes in Salt Lake City at the University of Phoenix in Utah. His interests include reading, writing (his writings include a published book), running, and travel—"a trip to Egypt and the Holy Land is a treasured memory," he says. David and his wife, Paula, have six children.

CHAPTER 12

Spiritual Survival: Feast or Famine

Kim M. Peterson

Eating is more than a habit, more than a social event, and more than a matter of routine; eating is necessary for survival. The meals we choose to eat may range from a casual snack to a formal dinner. The choice of what and where we eat is a luxury that some don't share.

Imagine receiving this invitation in the mail:

> You and a guest are cordially invited
> to an evening of fine dining
> *in your honor*
> at an internationally acclaimed
> Five-Star French Restaurant.
> R.S.V.P.

How lucky can you get? A flurry of issues would rush through your mind. Whom will you invite? What will you wear? Why are you so lucky? There would be no doubt that preparations must begin almost immediately.

With great anticipation, you and your friend drive up to the restaurant. The valet parks your car, the maitre d' greets you in the waiting area and shows you to your table. You can't help but notice the hewn-oak table thick with lacquer, the oak chairs, the fine china, the white linen, the delicate crystal, and the ornate silver. With calculated movements you sit down and survey the scene.

What you see is completely unlike the normal fast-food cuisine of cardboard and soda pop. Even the appetizers are a meal. French crackle bread sprinkled with sesame seeds and topped with butter, water served in a crystal pitcher with a slice of lemon, and French rolls, are indeed appetizing.

After a short wait and the disposal of the appetizers, the waitress offers you the soup: French onion soup. It does not take long to recognize that this is not freeze-dried soup from a packet. The savory broth is poured over whole slices of onions on top of French bread and Swiss cheese. As you cut through the saturated bread, your mouth begins to water. This is what eating should be!

When the soup is spent, the waitress returns with the salad: a fresh spinach salad with a vinaigrette dressing, bacon chips, and slices of boiled eggs and cucumbers. Even if you don't normally like salad, your curiosity drives you to taste this masterpiece. Spinach never tasted like this when your mom was forcing you to eat it.

Hors d'oeuvres follow the salad. Your eyes get wider as the waitress sets before you a plate of sautéed, stuffed mushrooms. Politely using the toothpick conveniently stuck in the bottom of the stuffed mushroom, you pick one up and quickly stuff your mouth with it. The spicy sausage, sour cream, chives, and buttery mushroom combine to create an exquisite taste sensation. You begin to weigh the cost of filling up on the hors d'oeuvres against the unquestionable value of leaving some room for the main course. With your limit set at three mushrooms, the waitress threatens to take the rest away. Quickly you determine that there is room for at least two more. Against the discretion of your better judgment, you decide to eat the last three mushrooms.

The spectacle reaches a peak when the waitress presents the main course: filet mignon. It is hard to conceive that food could be so picturesque. The round, twelve-ounce steak, wrapped in bacon, is surrounded by asparagus spears smothered in cheese and baby potatoes sautéed in butter. Cautiously you set your knife on the meat. Unlike the normal fare, this steak seems so tender that the knife glides through the filet easily. Your taste buds savor every bite. The main course fulfills your every expectation.

Even if you were forced to eat asparagus as a child, you eagerly try these asparagus spears. Somehow these vegetables are not like the frozen ones your mother prepared.

Satiation approaches. In an attempt to savor the final few bites of food, you chew more slowly. From the periphery of your view you notice the waitress approaching. In your mind you anticipate the dilemma she is about to present. Swallowing the last few bites, you contemplate your options. The waitress asks how everything was. You reply that it was wonderful. Then she asks if you would like dessert. Now, during your whole life you have liked dessert. You believe in your heart that you would like dessert now . . . but you are not sure that you have any room left in your digestive system. Ultimately you reason that you won't have another opportunity for French dessert, so you reply that you would like some chocolate mousse.

You welcome the five-minute wait for dessert. Maybe the food will begin to digest; maybe it will at least settle in your stomach. When the waitress sets the crystal dessert dish in front of you your appetite quickly returns. Unlike the instant pudding chocolate mousse that your mother made for snacks when you came home from school, this culinary delight is authentic. The thick, brown, creamy mousse is topped with a "globule" of real whipped cream. Shavings of real Swiss chocolate adorn the top of the whipped cream. The maraschino cherry is the perfect accent for the dessert.

Calculating carefully, you manage to get the cherry, several chocolate shavings, some whipped cream, and the creamy mousse in one scoop. As the dessert hits your mouth, previously unused taste buds quickly recognize the new taste and texture. Your final eating strategy is to let the mousse melt, slide down your throat, and seep between the cracks in your full stomach.

What an event! Most of us have experienced being full, but if you have ever been full of five-star, internationally acclaimed French food you will certainly remember it. This "all-you-can-eat" world of food is a sharp contrast to the "what-you-can-find" world of hunger.

As a missionary in Thailand, I saw starvation first-hand. One day, as my companion and I approached a bus stop, I couldn't help but notice a woman sitting with her back against the bus stop pole. Her hair was matted, her clothes were tattered, and she was begging for food.

My companion and I drew near. When the woman noticed us, the intensity of her begging increased. She reached out her wrinkled, dry hand. Her face was little more than a skeleton with skin stretched over it. The most shocking scene, however, was her twelve-year-old son, who lay limp in her arms. His bloated stomach, sunken eye sockets, and feeble limbs were reminiscent of commercials I had seen on television.

In light of the balanced meals that I had eaten that day, I could hardly pass by the two of them. I reached in my pocket and gave the woman twenty baht (the equivalent of one U.S. dollar). To my surprise, the starving mother lay on the sidewalk with her face in the cement and said, "You are a prince." Imagine that! Prior to my mission I was working for six dollars an hour; in ten minutes I could earn a dollar. For my giving her the equivalent of ten minutes' worth of work, this woman thought I was a prince. What a humbling experience!

Starvation is a worldwide dilemma; a startling number of people starve each year. The Lord assures us that there are plenty of resources available in this earth to support mankind: "For the earth is full, and there is enough and to spare." In the words which follow, the Lord warns us that our agency may be used to waste those resources: "Yea, I prepared all things, and have given unto the children of men to be agents unto themselves" (D&C 104:17).

The ultimate consequence of starvation is death. Spiritual rather than physical starvation, however, has the more significant consequence. What a tragedy! Within this world there are individuals who cannot find enough food to sustain their life. More tragic still are the Latter-day Saints who starve spiritually when they have the opportunity to feast.

Nephi invites us to "feast upon the words of Christ" (2 Nephi 32:3), but how do you feast on the scriptures? If you were invited to a feast like the one described earlier, you would be excited. In contrast, many Latter-day Saints are not excited about the scriptures. I have heard several teenagers explain that the scriptures are not exciting. Consider the following:

"The scriptures are boring." Eating is also boring. You always do the same thing: first you cut your food, then you stab it, then you chew it, then you swallow it. The fact that eating is repetitious, however, does not keep you from doing it.

"I don't understand the scriptures." I'm not sure that many of us

understand how the carbohydrates, proteins, and other nutrients in the food we eat interact with the enzymes in our stomachs to be broken down, absorbed by the blood, and carried to different parts of our bodies. If your mother, however, gave you a slice of chocolate cake you would appear silly if you said, "Mom, I don't think I want any cake because I don't understand how it will be absorbed into my bloodstream."

"I don't have time to read the scriptures." Can you imagine using lack of time as an excuse for not eating! If you had three very busy days back to back during which you didn't eat, you would probably faint. Having been rushed to the hospital, can you imagine saying to your nurse, "I'm sorry, I don't have time for an IV." If you don't have time to eat right now, you will probably make time in the near future.

It is sad if our attitude toward the scriptural feast is more like an attitude toward spiritual left-overs. My mother used to save left-overs from each meal. Saturday afternoon she would pull the left-overs from the refrigerator, reheat them, and give us left-overs for lunch. I hated that meal. You could get spaghetti with beans in it or tuna fish casserole with soggy potato-chip topping or mushy squash.

One Saturday afternoon my brothers and I refused to eat the left-overs. My mother calmly excused us from the table. The next day, Sunday, we came with great anticipation to eat the Sunday meal. (The dread of the "Saturday afternoon left-over meal" was always balanced by the anticipation of the "Sunday afternoon feast.") To our dismay, my mother pulled out her biggest casserole dish. In it she had mixed the spaghetti, the beans, the squash, the tuna fish casserole (complete with soggy potato chips on top). I learned that day that my mother considered all the food to be valuable.

Some of us treat the scriptures like left-overs. We think that, since we already know the story, what possible purpose could there be in reading them again? We know that in the Book of Mormon all of the Nephites die (sorry if I gave the story ending away for any of you). We know that in the Old Testament the Jews are scattered. In the New Testament the Savior dies and is resurrected. (Sometimes we are not sure what the book of Revelation is about.) What possible reason could there be to read the story if you already know the ending?

Sometimes the feast is not found in the story. Consider the

story of Nephi returning to get the brass plates. Most of us readily recognize that Nephi traveled a great distance, lost the precious things from his father's estate, and was tormented by Laman and Lemuel. We are familiar with the story of Laban being drunk in the streets of Jerusalem. We may even remember that Nephi did not want to kill Laban.

We may begin feasting when we ask why Nephi chose to tell us that story. Is it because Nephi wanted to show us that the scriptures were valuable to him? Did Nephi want us to know that he obeyed his father? Maybe the most exciting spiritual feast comes when we realize that Nephi was "led by the Spirit, not knowing beforehand the things which [he] should do" (1 Nephi 4:6). Hidden within a familiar story is a wonderful spiritual feast: we can allow the Spirit to direct our every action.

Frequently we choose only to "snack" on the feast that is set before us. Like a physical snack, a spiritual snack will only keep us satisfied momentarily. Some indications of spiritual snacking might include falling asleep while reading the scriptures, allowing only a few minutes for scripture study each day, or not making any significant changes as a result of scripture study. While each of these alternatives is better than not studying the scriptures at all, they hardly represent the scriptural feast to which we are invited.

If you are interested in breaking the "spiritual snack" habit, you might consider the following suggestions:

1. Devote some of your quality time to scripture study (e.g., a time when you are not sleepy).
2. Don't limit the amount of time that you dedicate to the scriptures. While setting a minimum goal of fifteen minutes each day is a valuable way to get in the habit of scripture study, you cannot expect to feast in fifteen minutes. Can you imagine trying to eat a seven-course meal in fifteen minutes?
3. Each time you read, try to find one thing that you could change in order to become more like Christ.

While an occasional candy bar is a nice break from normal meals, surviving on candy would be an unpleasant experience. Spiritual survival requires more than scriptural snacks.

If you were invited to a feast and were able to take a friend, you would choose someone with whom you had a good relationship. When you truly desire to "feast upon the words of Christ," it will become necessary to invite the Holy Ghost. Moroni suggests that "by the power of the Holy Ghost, [we] may know the truth of all things" (Moroni 10:5).

Unlike the tragedy of physical starvation, spiritual survival is your choice. If you have access to this book, you also have access to the scriptures. You may choose to feast by regularly searching the scriptures, trying to apply them to your life, and inviting the Holy Ghost to bear record of the truths they contain.

Kim M. Peterson is a seminary instructor living in Salt Lake City, Utah. He holds a master's degree in Human Resource Development from Brigham Young University. Kim enjoys skiing (he is a PSIA Level II ski instructor), fishing, photography, and cooking. He likes working with youth groups and admires their strength. Kim and his wife, Terri, are the parents of two children.

CHAPTER 13

Preparing for Celestial Marriage, or May I Water Your Camels, Please

Jack Marshall

When you first start dating at the golden, promising age of sixteen or older, you should commence on this exciting path always with the end in mind—the temple! The house of the Lord, his home on earth! Some of the words the Lord uses to describe marriage in his House are *everlasting, sealed, promise, power, dominion* (see D&C 132). Doesn't that sound inspiring? That sounds a whole lot better than marriage solemnized at the Chapel of Eternal Bliss and Casino on the Las Vegas strip!

One of the finest scriptural examples of dating with the end in mind or preparation for marital bliss is found in the account of Isaac and Rebekah as they prepared for marriage (see Genesis 24).

The time had come for father Abraham to select a wife for his son Isaac. As Abraham sent a servant to find Isaac a companion, he admonished him to "swear by the Lord, the God of heaven, and the God of the earth, that thou shalt not take a wife unto my son of the daughters of the Canaanites, among whom I dwell" (Genesis 24:3). The great patriarch that Abraham was is shown here as he stresses emphatically that his son is to begin this tremendous challenge and adventure of marriage with a partner who will enhance and strengthen his sacred beliefs, not restrict or weaken them. Isaac's wife was to be a faithful member.

As a brand-new father I had a memorable experience that reinforced this idea.

I stood in the dinner line leading to the hospital cafeteria and reflected on the events of the last hour. It had been the most rewarding time that I had yet experienced in my life. Just moments ago, my first son had been born.

A boy! A son! My pal! I envisioned future campouts, hikes, wrestling together, and of course all-state pitching honors on his high school baseball team. We would start practicing immediately after his three-day hospital recovery from his trip down the birth canal. A son! He was awesome! A beautiful boy! Well, not quite beautiful; ugly would be more fitting. All little babies are ugly when born. They have a resemblance to the Pillsbury dough boy, and if that weren't scary enough they have horrendously wrinkled skin, since they've spent the last nine months immersed in water. Nevertheless, he was awesome, and if his looks didn't improve we could always put his baby bonnet on backwards.

My day-dreaming was interrupted by a faint, off-tune whistle that drew closer to me from behind. I glanced over my shoulder and saw a freckle-faced girl of about nine years old, with straggly blond hair falling loosely over her faded jacket. Oblivious to me, she walked past and nonchalantly cut in front of me in the line without missing a note of her tune. I was fourth in line from the front. I looked down at her and thought to myself, "You little brat!" Not really! Nothing could erase the warm glow of happiness that the past hour had brought, not even a somewhat rude little child.

We moved slowly toward the serving area. The whistled tune stopped abruptly, and in a commanding voice she said, "You eat with me, okay?"

I smiled down at this strange little girl. "It would be a pleasure."

Without any acknowledgement she continued down the line, stopping momentarily to position her tray, which she awkwardly knocked against the tray slide that was almost level with her nose. Speaking to one of the cooks, she said, "I want some of that and that and that." He dished up a plate of tuna casserole and some green beans. As we neared the dessert section she pointed to a dish of vanilla ice cream and, addressing me, said, "Hand me that." I obeyed. Her final "request," made in a demanding voice, was for a glass of milk that she was unable to reach. At the cashier's stand her bill totaled two dollars and ten cents. Quickly she handed the young lady a couple of wrinkled dollar bills she had clutched in her hand. The cashier politely inquired about the remaining dime. Her reply was simple and to the point. "I don't have any more money" and off she went. I hurriedly located two nickels in my pocket and handed them to the perplexed cashier.

My young companion lifted her unyielding tray, which swayed back and forth, sloshing her milk. Calling to me over her shoulder, she commanded, "Follow me." As we seated ourselves she introduced herself. "My name is Janelle. Now tell me yours."

"Jack," I replied.

"It's nice to meet you," she responded, as she took her first and only bite of her tuna casserole. She then scooped up a spoonful of ice cream. Stopping with it short of her mouth, she fixed her dark brown eyes on a banana I had purchased with my meal. "I like bananas on my ice cream," she said. Being a banana lover myself, I reluctantly peeled the banana and even sliced it over her ice cream. She gobbled that up at warp speed, then began scanning my tray to see what else I had to offer. I started eating faster!

As we neared the end of our meal, curiosity led me to question Janelle. "What are you doing at the hospital this late at night." It was nine-thirty. "Are you waiting for someone?"

Without a moment's hesitation she replied: "I'm eating. Mommy doesn't usually fix dinner for me. We only live three blocks from here, so she gives me money to come here and eat."

Janelle finished her ice cream and, surveying my dinner tray, focused on a piece of German chocolate cake. I could have pantomimed her words. "I like chocolate cake." With the aid of my knife, one piece became two. With cake crumbs clinging to her lips she said, "You're nice, Jack."

When I had finished my dinner I thanked Janelle for being a delightful dinner companion and got up to leave. As I turned to leave, I felt a tug on my coat. I looked back at Janelle. Her countenance had changed. With a voice bordering on begging she spoke. "Can't you stay longer and visit with me?" It hit me all of a sudden like a two by four between the eyes that Janelle probably came often by herself to eat, finding someone to share the occasion with.

I had been anxious to get upstairs to the nursery and hold my awesome new son, but I was torn between being with my boy and the lonely request of my new, attention-starved little friend. "Ten minutes is as long as I can stay, okay?"

Contented, she continued eating and visiting. The time passed quickly. We said good-bye again and shook hands. As I got up to leave, she held my hand tightly. "Won't you please stay?" I explained that I really had to leave to be with my wife and my baby boy. "That's nice you have a new baby, Jack." Slowly, reluctantly she released my hand.

As I turned to go she pointed to an elderly couple seated across the room. "Do you think they'll eat with me if I ask?"

I groaned sympathetically within. "I bet they will."

Janelle was satisfied. She arose and lifted her tray and made her way to the table where the couple sat. As I walked away from the sounds of clanging dishes and busy conversations that are common to cafeterias and restaurants, I could hear above it all a little girl's voice saying, a little less commandingly, "You eat with me, okay?"

You might ask what this story has to do with Abraham's desire for his son to marry within the Church. The gospel of Jesus Christ teaches us how to be successful in fulfilling our greatest responsibilities we'll have on earth, that of husbands, wives, and parents. Family requires much sacrifice. A couple has to be united and committed in their beliefs if they are to create an environment within their home where the family will flourish with love and attention. Having the same basic beliefs and working together with those beliefs is the key. Creating this foundation starts years before marriage in choosing whom you will date.

President Spencer W. Kimball wrote: "Clearly, right marriage begins with right dating. . . . Therefore, this warning comes with great emphasis. Do not take the chance of dating nonmembers, or members who are untrained and faithless. [You] may say, 'Oh, I do not intend to marry this person. It is just a "fun" date.' But one cannot afford to take a chance on falling in love with someone who may never accept the gospel." (*The Miracle of Forgiveness* [Salt Lake City: Bookcraft, 1969], pp. 241-42.) If you choose to date a person who does not maintain LDS standards, you are not on that account a horrible sinner! But you are taking a risk of jeopardizing future happiness and fulfillment.

It is an inalienable right of each child born into this world to have parents prepared to take care of his many needs. Parents can do this only if they are unified and are headed in the same direction. Thus it's critically important that they have the same belief system.

Abraham's servant left in search for one who believed as devotedly as Isaac.

As the servant arrived in the land of Abraham's kin, he prayed, "O Lord God of my master Abraham, I pray thee, send me good speed this day, and show kindness unto my master Abraham. Behold, I stand here by the well of water; and the daughters of the men of the city come out to draw water; and let it come to pass, that the damsel to whom I shall say, Let down thy pitcher, I pray thee, that I may drink; and she shall say, Drink, and I will give thy camels drink also: let the same be she that thou hast appointed for thy servant Isaac." (Genesis 24:12-14.)

The wisdom of this servant is shown as he senses the inadequacy of his own wisdom and seeks the Lord's guidance in his weighty assignment. If each of us, like Abraham's servant, would seek to have the Lord's seal of approval upon our dating activities and prospective mates, and his assistance in becoming a good catch, it would mean a lot less heartache in dating and marriage.

A classic story of one who sought the Lord's assistance and approval is found in the story of Sarah Pea, who became the wife of Elder Charles C. Rich, one of the early apostles. In March 1837 some Elders, while passing through the area in which the Peas lived, stayed at Sarah's home. It is recorded in the biography of Charles Rich that one of these Elders said to her one day, "Sarah, I have taken the liberty of recommending you to a very fine young man, who I believe would make you a good companion." Then he told her the young man's name, Charles Rich. A few months later another missionary, while talking to the Peas about "gathering" to Missouri, suddenly turned to Sarah and remarked, "I have a good young elder picked out for you." To her surprise, he too gave her the name of Elder Rich.

About a month after this last conversation, Sarah was told there was a letter at the post office for her father. Her father was not at home at the time, so she mounted a horse and went for it. On opening the letter, she found one on the inside addressed to her. It was from the young man whose name had been mentioned to her several times as a possible husband. Imagine her surprise when she read the following epistle: "Miss Sarah Pea. It is with pleasure that I at this time pen a few lines to you, although a perfect stranger to you. However, I trust that these few lines may be received by you, and may be the beginning of a happy acquaintance with you. I will now let you know the reason for my boldness in writing to you. It is because Elder G. M. Hinkle and others have highly recommended you as a Saint of the last days, as being worthy of my attention. I think I should be happy to get a good companion, such a one as I could take comfort with through life, and such a one as could take comfort with me. As you have been recommended to me as such, I should be very happy to see you and converse with you on the subject."

Can you believe that letter? Sounds just like a business deal, like he's buying a horse—she's got good teeth, strong back, good hoofs, I'll take her. The letter continues:

"I have understood from Brother Hinkle that you were going up to Zion this spring or summer. I should be happy to see you there, and if these lines are received with the same feeling that I write them, I trust that you may be single and unengaged. When this comes to hand and after you read and meditate upon it, I should be glad if you would write me an answer to it.

"Yours with the best of respects, Charles C. Rich."

Obviously, Charles Rich was not a bashful kind of guy.

Well, what would you do if you got such a letter? Pray, right? Sarah desired to receive a confirmation concerning the letter she had received. She sought the Lord's help. One day shortly after the letter came, Sarah was reading the Bible. Her eye caught a verse in the book of Ruth as she read it, and the Spirit descended upon her like a ton of bricks, confirming to her that this was her answer. She immediately penned what she had read and mailed it to Brother Rich. Her letter read: "Mr. Charles C. Rich: Intreat me not to leave thee, or to return from following after thee: for whither thou goest, I will go; and where thou lodgest, I will lodge: thy people shall be my people, and thy God my God: where thou diest, will I die, and there will I be buried: the Lord do so to me, and more also, if ought but death part thee and me [Ruth 1:16-17]. With great respect, I remain Yours truly, Sarah Pea."

Is that awesome or what!

We later learn from Sarah: "It was about six months after this, before my father sold his property and moved to Missouri. And it was about two weeks before I met the young man Charles C. Rich. It was at a public meeting that we first saw each other. Without any one pointing us out to each other, we knew each other at sight. In four months from this time we were married." (John Henry Evans, *Charles Coulson Rich, Pioneer Builder of the West* [New York: Macmillan, 1936], pp. 41-43.) It may not always happen that dramatically, but we can be assured that the Lord will reveal his will if we do our part.

Sarah and Elder Charles Rich were a great strength and support to one another through many difficulties faced by the Saints in the early years of the Church. It seems that much of the strength and support they experienced had its origin from the knowledge that their courtship and marriage had their Heavenly Father's assistance and approval from the beginning.

As we continue the story of Rebekah and Isaac, we read that before the servant of Abraham had finished his plea with the Lord, "Rebekah came out . . . with her pitcher upon her shoulder. And the damsel was very fair to look upon, a virgin, neither had any man known her." (Genesis 24:15-16.) A great message is contained in these verses. Verse 16 says Rebekah was fair to look upon. Many might interpret this to mean she was physically an attractive person, and rightfully so. But I believe the next part of the sentence states why Rebekah's countenance was so fair to look upon: "a virgin, neither had any man known her."

We live in a time when many young people are misled by society's standards of what beauty is, whether it be an attractive figure, stylish clothes, or the latest hairstyle. True beauty of womanhood and noble manhood are derived from honoring the sacred law of chastity. Rebekah was honoring this law.

The story continues: "The servant ran to meet her, and said, Let me, I pray thee, drink a little water of thy pitcher. And she said, Drink, my lord. And she hasted, and let down her pitcher upon her hand, and gave him drink. And when she was done giving him drink, she said, I will draw water for thy camels also, until they have done drinking. And she hasted, and emptied her pitcher into the trough, and ran again unto the well to draw water, and drew for all his camels." (Genesis 24:17-20.)

Rebekah's actions here display an important attribute of preparation for a celestial marriage—service. Rebekah had developed herself to be a giving and unselfish person, ready to serve her God through serving others. This is indicated by several words in verse 20. She hasted (meaning she went quickly and eagerly) and she ran (an indication of a desire to please through service). She watered all the stranger's camels, not stopping short of being complete in her service to a brother.

This service was no easy or blissful task either. There were ten thirsty, smelly, slobbering camels. I've heard that a camel takes about fifty gallons before it reaches the full mark.

Though centuries would pass before the Savior's birth, Rebekah had internalized his words: "Verily I say unto you, Inasmuch as ye have done it unto one of the least of these my brethren, ye have done it unto me" (Matthew 25:40).

If you're really serious about developing yourself, service will be one of the greatest attributes you can concentrate on.

The servant learned Rebekah's identity, went with her to meet her family, and conveyed the unique story to a perplexed brother and the mother of Rebekah. The next morning Abraham's servant was anxious to be off on the return journey. Her brother and her mother wanted him to wait, to take it easy for a few days. They said: "Let the damsel abide with us a few days, at the least ten; after that she shall go." He replied, "Hinder me not, seeing the Lord hath prospered my way; send me away that I may go to my master." And they said, "We will call the damsel, and enquire at her mouth. And they called Rebekah, and said unto her, Wilt thou go with this man?" (Genesis 24:56-58.)

Rebekah's simple reply teaches us another vital step in preparing oneself for celestial marriage—faith in our Heavenly Father. Her reply, "I will go" (Genesis 24:58), is reminiscent of a well-used statement of Nephi's: "I, Nephi, said unto my father: I will go and do the things which the Lord hath commanded, for I know that the Lord giveth no commandments unto the children of men, save he shall prepare a way for them that they may accomplish the thing which he commandeth them" (1 Nephi 3:7). Part of the credit for this classic scripture might well be given to Nephi's great, great . . . grandmother Rebekah, who in a time of decision and a test of faith manifested an acute sensitivity to the Spirit and said, "I will go."

Finally Rebekah and Isaac meet. Notice the sequence in verse 67: "And Isaac brought her into his mother Sarah's tent, and took Rebekah, and she became his wife; and he loved her." A great moral contained here teaches us to marry someone we can love before marriage but, more important, after marriage. Don't let infatuation or physical attraction blind you to the kind of person you're considering spending eternity with. In other words, it is best to go into marriage with your eyes open and then close them after you have married, rather than go into it with your eyes shut and open them afterwards.

In a day when love, infatuation, and physical attraction are believed to be synonymous, it would be well to teach that true and lasting love, or celestial love, comes from years of tender mutual care (see Genesis 24:67).

We might ask, "What truly are the benefits of proper preparation for a celestial marriage?" A great answer is contained in Doctrine and Covenants 132:37: "Isaac also and Jacob did none other things than that which they were commanded; and because they did none other things than that which they were commanded, they have entered into their exaltation, according to the promises, and sit upon thrones, and are not angels but are gods." After four thousand years of marriage, Rebekah sits on a throne at the side of her husband, Isaac. She has provided us with an excellent example of how to prepare for a celestial marriage—in her case one that started long ago and continues because of her following a few time-tested rules: marry a faithful individual within the Church; seek approval through the Spirit; be a pure person; learn to serve others; develop great faith; and go into marriage with your eyes open.

Jack Marshall is director of the institute of religion in Glendora, California. He holds a master's degree in Education from Brigham Young University. Jack enjoys racquetball, baseball, and camping. He has lived in the Philippines, Japan, and Johnston Island (a small island in the Pacific measuring one mile long and a half-mile wide). Jack and his wife, Liz, are the parents of five children.

CHAPTER 14

Receiving Spiritual Guidance During the Teen Years

Randal A. Wright

Several years ago I published a magazine that focused on Mormon athletes. Occasionally we would let the athletes write their own stories for publication. I was very impressed with one that was written by Henry Marsh, one of Brigham Young University's great track stars. Henry was a college All-American in cross-country and track; the American record holder in the steeplechase; a Pan-American Game winner and later a member of the U.S. Olympic team. He began his article with the following story:

"Hello! My name is Henry D. Marsh. I was named after my grandfather Henry D. Moyle, who was President David O. McKay's First Counselor [in the First Presidency]. Henry D. Moyle's grandfather was James Moyle, who crossed the Atlantic Ocean and the plains after being converted to the Mormon church in Cornwall, England. He later became the superintendent of construction of Temple Square in Salt Lake City. I am grateful for my heritage and their strong testimonies. My life was saved because of my grandfather's closeness to the Lord.

"When I was about a year old I was at my grandfather's house while he was very sick with shingles. He had not been out of bed for a week, and he was not supposed to get out. However, something prompted him to get up immediately and go to the backyard. It was there that he found me drowning in his fish pond. I had hit my head and was lying face down in the water. My lungs were full of water, and mouth-to-mouth resuscitation was quickly administered. The Fire Department was also called in to assist. At that time I was given a blessing by Harold B. Lee, who was a close friend of my grandfather's. I am here today because my grandfather lived a life worthy of the companionship of the Holy Ghost." (*Mormon Sport*, January 1980, p. 8.)

Why did President Moyle get out of his sick bed at exactly the right time to save his young grandson from death? Obviously President Moyle was very close to the Spirit and he knew that he should follow the prompting without hesitation. Our Church authorities are very spiritual men, but you do not have to be a General Authority to experience the guidance of the Holy Ghost in your life. This gift is available to all who are willing to pay the price. Having the Holy Ghost to guide our lives is one of the greatest gifts we could ever receive. Elder Lorenzo Snow gave these comforting words: "God . . . has . . . conferred upon us his Holy Spirit, which is an unerring guide, standing, as an angel of God, at our side, telling us what to do, and affording us strength and succor when adverse circumstances arise in our way" (*Journal of Discourses* 20:191).

Just think about that promise. In every situation you could know exactly what decision to make. Being a teenager can be quite challenging and frustrating at times. It's a time of ever-increasing temptations. It can be a time of joy and happiness or one of sorrow and regret. Often the determining factor will be how well our lives are in tune with the Spirit.

Two years ago I was sitting in my office at the Lamar University Institute in Beaumont, Texas, when a young lady I'd never seen before walked in. She said she was a freshman student at the university and wanted to learn a little more about our church. We arranged for her to return at 12:15 P.M. the next day.

At 9:15 A.M. the following day she showed up again. I was right in the middle of something very important and had not expected her to be three hours early. She said that she had "this feeling" that she should come at that time instead of the appointed time. Since I could not really spend any time with her, I took her down into the classroom to let her watch the film *The First Vision*. Just when I got the TV set up, the classroom door opened and in walked two full-time missionaries. They said they had never been into the institute before, but as they were driving to an important appointment they both had a very strong feeling to turn around and stop at the institute. They walked in at the very moment they were needed. Their visit and the girl's early arrival could not have been a coincidence.

The missionaries immediately formed a friendship with Jennifer and were able to set up an appointment with her for the following week. Well, you might guess the rest of the story. Jennifer joined the Church and is now engaged to be married in the temple to a returned missionary. Why? Because two young Elders were led by the Spirit to a young lady who was searching for the truth.

How would it be to have this great source guiding every decision you made? How would it be to have help with every teenage problem that you will face? It is possible if we are worthy to receive it.

This is an exciting time to be alive, yet it can be quite frightening because of the many temptations and challenges you face. You need the Holy Spirit's guidance to help you through the trying times of your teen years. Whether your challenge is losing important games, sub-standard grades, not making the team, a bad complexion, weight, or whatever, you can have help if you turn to the Spirit. As President Marion G. Romney pointed out, "The key to happiness is to get the Spirit and keep it" (in Conference Report, October 1961, p. 61).

How can we bring this spirit into our lives and receive the great blessings associated with this gift? First we must realize that it will require work to obtain these blessings. President Wilford Woodruff pointed out: "Every man and woman in this Church should *labor* to get that Spirit. We are surrounded by these evil spirits that are at war against God and against everything looking to the building up of the kingdom of God; and we need this Holy Spirit to enable us to overcome these influences." (*Deseret Weekly*, 7 November 1896, p. 643.)

Following are some of the things we can do to help us have the Spirit in our lives.

Pray

Over the years I have had the opportunity of hearing many youth bear their testimonies. I remember a priest in a midwestern state who was a star football player for a team *USA Today* ranked among the nation's top five teams. He told about an experience he had as his team played for the state championship. He was sitting at the back of the bus traveling to the game when he decided to offer a silent prayer of thanks for the great opportunities he was having. He said that as he began to pray he experienced a feeling of peace such as he had never felt before. He began to cry because of these wonderful feelings. Then a small voice whispered that his team would lose the game that day, but that that was okay and he was loved. His teammates wanted to know what was wrong with him, but he couldn't tell them what he was feeling. They assumed he was just nervous about the game.

The game was a very hard-fought one, but in the end his team lost, just as he knew they would. After the game he was still filled with happiness because of his spiritual experience. He was the only member of his team who was not crying. He felt totally at peace as he congratulated the members of the opposing team. This young man had experienced what the Lord promised when he said, "My Spirit . . . shall fill your soul with joy" (D&C 11:13). When you have the Spirit in your life even great disappointment can mean peace. President Ezra Taft Benson gave great counsel that will help with any challenge you face: "From simple trials to our Gethsemanes, prayer can put us in touch with God, our greatest source of comfort and counsel" (in Conference Report, October 1974, p. 91).

Put Spiritual Reminders in Your Bedroom

Over the years I have stayed overnight in many homes when I have been out on the speaking circuit, often in the home of one of the stake leaders. More often than not I stay in a teenager's bedroom. It's interesting how closely this youth's spirituality seems to match his or her bedroom. In some rooms I see large posters of rock stars, movie stars, and athletes. Sometimes I see magazines and books lying around. Often I have seen nice stereo systems with large record collections. Very seldom have I observed a youth whose room did not match his countenance.

I'll never forget the room of a beautiful girl in a southern state. On her desk was a copy of the Book of Mormon, along with several other Church books. On her walls were the pictures of several temples and Mormon Ads from the *New Era*. Also hanging on her wall in a beautiful frame were her life goals. These included items like:

I will learn to play the piano

I will earn my Young Womanhood award

I will not date until I am sixteen

I will pray morning and night

I will read the scriptures daily

I will marry in the temple

I will be an honor student

Obviously this girl put the gospel of Jesus Christ at the center of her life. Did she match her room? Yes, she was one of the most impressive girls I have ever met.

If I were to visit your room, what would I find on the walls, the bulletin board, or your nightstand? What kind of records or cassettes would I find? If you want the Spirit in your life, in your bedroom put reminders of who you are and what you stand for.

Ask What Jesus Would Do

For the past several years I have had the great opportunity of serving as a co-director for sessions of Especially for Youth. During my August 1991 session I gave every counselor and participant a wooden nickel to keep in his pocket. Engraved on this nickel was the message, "What would Jesus do?" Recipients were told to think about this little reminder with every decision they made.

Asking this question can be a great benefit. After the session some of the EFY counselors took a religion class from me. For one of their assignments they were to try to live for a week asking "What would Jesus do?" in every situation they were faced with. They kept a daily journal of their experiences. Following are two brief accounts of experiences they had that help point out ways to bring the Spirit into our lives:

Treat Others with Kindness and Respect

1. "There was this girl in one of my classes whom I had seen before. She doesn't talk to anyone in class, wears a frown most of

the day, and would be considered a 'sweet spirit,' I guess. As we left class I walked next to her and introduced myself. She smiled as I spoke to her. We talked as we walked to our classes, which weren't together but were in the same building.

"I found out she was a very interesting person. Not only did we have a lot in common but also we knew a lot of the same people. At first I thought I was doing her a favor, but as I reflected more on this situation I knew I was doing myself a favor by getting to know this girl and making a new friend. If I did this once a day, or once a week, the amount of new friendships I could form would be countless. When we do as Jesus would do, we can feel the Spirit in our lives and we feel happy."

Be friendly to those you associate with. Don't judge them without even knowing them. Many people are lonely and depressed and lost. By treating others with kindness and respect you help bring the Spirit into your own life.

Forgive Those Who Have Wronged You

2.   "Tonight will be a night I will never forget. The day started off well. I went to work, and while I was there I tried to figure out what I was going to do for my date tonight. It was the first date with a girl I have known since summer. We've done things together before, but never as a formal date. I finally decided what I was going to do, and I spent a couple of hours getting things ready. It wasn't going to be just a dinner and a movie. I had planned what I considered to be my most creative date.

"I was really excited both to see her and to carry out my plans. I thought that tonight was going to be the funniest date I had ever had. Boy, was I wrong! The whole night she was a brat. No matter what I did, she wouldn't respond. It was as if she was determined not to have a good time. To make a long and very depressing story short, the night ended with her telling me how much of a jerk I was, how conceited, selfish, and pig-headed.

"I had never had a date turn out like that. I was so angry I couldn't speak. The only thing I wanted was to get rid of her. Then, all of a sudden, I thought about the question—'What would Jesus do?' What bad timing! I had every right to be angry and even feel a little sorry for myself, but I couldn't. I don't know what it was exactly. I know that I never read a scripture that said that Jesus went out out on a date, let alone go through the same experience, but I felt like Jesus wouldn't have reacted that way. I felt justified in my anger. I had tried so hard to impress her and help her to have a good time, yet she slammed me hard. Still I couldn't be angry. Tonight I learned that forgiving and forgetting, even when the offender doesn't ask for it, is what Jesus would do. Oh well, so there's one less girl to go out with.

[Four days later] "Guess what I did today? I put my pride in my back pocket and did something that my best friends thought I shouldn't have. Well, do you remember that date Saturday night? I realized that there's more to it than forgiving and forgetting. I had to work through it. I realized that if I were to see this girl at school, I don't think we would talk to each other. At first, I felt self-justified in that she was the mean one, that I hadn't done anything wrong, in fact I had even forgiven her without her asking. But that wasn't enough. I had to do something to make amends even if she wasn't going to. So I got a rose, put a little joke on the card, and sent it to her via a friend. I didn't expect any reply. I was just content feeling that I had done what Christ would have done had he been in my place. It's kind of hard to explain how I feel, but I picture Christ being made fun of and mocked yet still he loved and served the people. What happened to me was nothing compared to what happened to him."

Here was a young man who felt the joy that comes when we forgive others. One of the real challenges of the teenage years is to not hold grudges against those who have wronged us. The Spirit comes strongly to those who can follow the example of the Savior in this area. If you want to have the Spirit to guide you in your life, ask yourself, "What would Jesus do?"

Use Quiet Times

One thing we must learn about the Holy Ghost is that he whispers his messages to us. We live in a fast-paced, noisy society. From the minute most teenagers get up in the morning until they go to bed at night there is almost nonstop noise. What with radio, television, movies, video games, and so on, little time is left for listening to the Spirit. One of the most rewarding things we can do is to spend some quiet time and just listen to what the Spirit whispers to us. Set aside some time to ask questions. Then just sit and write the answers you receive.

For example we may ask, "How can I be a better person? How can I have more friends? How can I be a better student?" After you have asked the questions, take the time to listen and record the answers that come to you. You will be amazed at the insights that will be revealed. Our Heavenly Father is waiting to help us with the challenges we face, but we must ask and listen quietly for the answers.

Act on What the Spirit Says

My great-grandfather William Williamson was born in New Orleans, Louisiana, in 1830. After serving for the Confederate Army during the Civil War, he moved to Texas with his wife, Joissine, in 1866. He had never joined any church, although he was a very religious man.

In January of 1900 two young missionaries got lost in the forests of east Texas and ended up knocking on his door. Shortly afterwards he and my great-grandmother joined the Church. He was seventy years old at the time and very ill. He died six months after his baptism, but his wife and children stayed close to the Church. William now has approximately two thousand descendants, over 90 percent of them members of the Church.

I was serving as the president of our family association when we decided to have a Texas State historical marker erected in William's honor, denoting him as an early Mormon pioneer in Texas. As we were meeting we looked at an old Book of Mormon that was left with the family back in 1900, and in it we found the names of the two missionaries who had taught them. Our family historian—an older sister named Arlen—said, "Wouldn't it be nice if we could contact the descendants of the two missionaries, Elder Reed from Spanish Fork, Utah, and Elder Brooks from Mesa, Arizona?" I called the Church Missionary Department, but they had no records on the missionaries who served in the Southern States Mission during 1899 and 1900.

At our next meeting I informed the committee that we would not be able to contact any of the two missionaries' descendants. Arlen didn't say much until the end of the meeting. Then she announced that she would try to find their descendants. I asked her how she planned to accomplish this task. She said she felt "inspired" to write to the postmaster in Mesa, Arizona, to ask him if he knew anyone there that was a descendant of Joseph Brooks, the missionary who served in Texas during 1899 and 1900. I tried not to laugh, but I thought that was one of the silliest ideas I had ever heard. How would the postmaster of such a large city know the descendants of a turn-of-the-century missionary?

Several weeks had passed when I received an excited phone call. "Guess what we have for our dedication service of the historical marker?" I had no idea what could be so exciting. "We have the personal missionary journals of Joseph Brooks, who helped convert William and Joissine to the Church. He tells the story of their conversion in these journals."

What good fortune! How did we get these journals? I soon learned that the Spirit can help guide our decisions, and that we must act on what the Spirit tells us to do. Our historian had written to the postmaster in Mesa as she had been prompted to do. He didn't know anyone named Brooks that may have been a descendant of the missionary. He did, however, know a lady named Mildred Jones that he thought was named Brooks before she was married. She no longer lived in Mesa, but he sent the letter to a forwarding address in Los Angeles, California. She did not live at that address anymore, either. The post office in California had a forwarding address in Phoenix, Arizona, so they sent the letter back. The letter finally reached a seventy-year-old sister, who turned out to be Joseph Brooks's daughter. She had been given her father's missionary journals. She was so excited to hear what had happened to the descendants of one of her father's converts that she sent the journals to our family organization to use in our ceremony. What an experience it was to read the actual account of my ancestors' conversion, written by the missionary who taught them!

What were the chances of that letter going to three different cities [with combined populations of millions] and reaching Joseph Brooks's daughter without the guidance of the Spirit? I have learned that if you are worthy and need answers to the challenges you face, "it shall be given by the Comforter, the Holy Ghost, that knoweth all things" (D&C 35:19).

But what good does it do to be inspired by the Holy Ghost and then not act on what we are inspired to do? What if our family historian had been inspired to write the letter but had not followed up on that feeling? We would never have had the great experience of reading the journals. We must act on what we are given.

Give Service

Another way to help bring the Spirit into our lives is through service. The prophets over the years have told us that. "If you would be happy, render a kind service, make somebody else happy" (David O. McKay, in Conference Report, October 1936, p. 104).

I challenged one of my religion classes at BYU to spend a week serving other people. The following is a journal entry from a former Especially for Youth counselor.

"Tonight I went to see a girl I met over the summer during EFY. She was a counselor in the Texas session and I was really excited to see her. When I arrived at her apartment she was on a long-distance phone conversation, so I just sat around and visited with her roommates. About the time she got off the phone, a young man came in asking if anyone could help him with his physics. He had a major test the next day and did not understand what he was doing. I had three choices before me: I could talk with my friend, which was the purpose of going to her apartment; I could go and help the young man with his physics; or I could talk briefly to my friend and get home and study for my own classes. I decided my friend would be there to visit with another time. My own physics test wasn't until the next Monday, so I could wait to study. Finally, the young man's physics test was tomorrow, and my help would mean so much to him. So I went and helped him with physics. Serving other people can sure bring a person great happiness."

Spiritual highs can leave you feeling good for days, months, and even years. When was the last time you served others without being asked?

Share Your Testimony

When you share your testimony with others it brings the Spirit into your life and often influences those you share it with. I had this reemphasized to me while speaking in a southern state. I stayed with the family of the stake Young Women president. She had a beautiful fifteen-year-old daughter named Chelsea. While there I was told a story about Chelsea sharing her testimony with her grandparents. Her grandmother was a member of the Church, but her grandfather, who was seventy-nine years old, had never joined. He had been through many sets of missionaries through the years, and most of his family had given up trying to convert him.

In 1988 Chelsea's grandparents paid her way to attend the "Academy for Girls" held at BYU. When she got home she felt inspired to write the following letter to her grandparents:

"Dear Grandma and Grandpa,

"Hello! How are you? I am fine. I just decided I'd write to tell you how grateful I am that you sent me to Academy for Girls. I had a great time. . . .

"On the last Wednesday we had a pizza party and a testimony meeting for two hours and forty-five minutes. I'd like to bear my testimony to you that I know this Church is true. I know that families can be together forever and that we were all friends up in the preexistence. We all have divine missions and were sent down to earth to fulfill them. I learned that if you know who you are, you can be the best you can be. I know that I am a child of God—we all are. He loves us and is pleased when we serve him. It is so important to be baptized and sealed in the temple. I want to be able to see you both as a family after we die. I go to the temple and do baptisms for the dead, but it's up to them whether they accept it or not.

"One of our speakers, Brad Wilcox, talked about being like children. He said we need to get back our self-esteem, happiness, love, wisdom, innocence, and faith. . . . As people get older they tend to get proud and lose their child-like faith. But to Heavenly Father and Mother we're still little children. We were sent here to succeed. He will help us succeed.

"I'm so glad that every morning and night I'm not ashamed to kneel down and pray to Father in Heaven. We all have our free agency and can choose what is right for us. I love you both and can tell you that my testimony was really strengthened there.

Love, Chelsea"

Chelsea's grandfather was so touched by the spirit of the letter that he was baptized soon after receiving it. A year later he was sealed to his wife in the Atlanta Temple.

Humble testimonies can change the lives of those who bear them and those who hear them. How many people would be brought into the Church if all the members truly lived by the Spirit and followed its promptings?

Youth living in today's world have many challenges to face. Satan is trying everything in his power to bring our youth down and ultimately destroy their earthly missions. But you can and will succeed! President Spencer W. Kimball has said: "Now, my young brothers [and sisters], remember that every David has a Goliath to defeat, and every Goliath can be defeated. He may not be a bully who fights with fists or sword or gun. He may not even be flesh and blood. He may not be nine feet tall; he may not be armor-protected, but every boy has his Goliaths. And every boy has access to the brook with its smooth stones.

"You will meet Goliaths who threaten you. Whether your Goliath is a town bully or is the temptation to steal or to destroy or the temptation to rob or the desire to curse or swear; if your Goliath is the desire to wantonly destroy or the temptation to lust and to sin, or the urge to avoid activity, whatever is your Goliath, he can be slain. But remember, to be the victor, one must follow the path that David followed: 'David behaved himself wisely in all his ways; and the Lord was with him' (1 Samuel 18:14)." (*The Teachings of Spencer W. Kimball* [Salt Lake City: Bookcraft, 1982], p. 154.)

And how do we "behave wisely in all his ways?" We live worthy of having the Holy Ghost as a companion, and, as Elray L. Christiansen said, "When the Holy Ghost is really within us, Satan must remain without" (in Conference Report, October 1974, p. 30).

Randal A. Wright, a religion instructor and a doctoral candidate at BYU, and former editor of a sports magazine, lists his interests and likes as speaking to the youth, waterparks, basketball, autobiographies, and country/Western music. He says the youth of today are "the royal generation saved to prepare the way for the Savior's return." Randal and his wife, Wendy, have five children.

CHAPTER 15

The War in Heaven Is Now Being Fought on Earth

Randall C. Bird

Quite a few years ago, while a junior in high school, I played in a football game that I vividly remember. Our high school, about eight hundred students, was playing one of the largest schools in the state of Idaho. This school happened to be rated number 2 in the state that year, and our coach posted clippings about the size of their team members. It just so happened that their defensive line averaged more man for man than Idaho State University's defensive line. Needless to say, we were the underdogs for this game.

The night of the game arrived, and we excitedly began our pre-game warm-ups—all twenty-seven of us. As we were partway through our warm-ups, the other team ran onto the field. It almost felt as if the field tilted in their direction. They were huge—all ninety-nine of them. They had good-looking uniforms with new helmets. We had the same old stuff that had been worn for years.

After finishing our warm-ups, we went into the locker room for our pre-game pep talk from the head coach. This is where you want to get motivated to go out there and defeat your opponent. Instead, our coach looked at us and said: "All right, guys, I know we can't win tonight, but would you at least put on a good show for our community." Now, doesn't that excite you! We went back onto the field to meet our Goliath with fear instead of with hope that we could win.

The captains met in the middle of the field for the coin toss to determine which team would kick and which team would receive. We won the toss. I felt it was the only thing we could win that night. We elected to receive the ball.

The opening kick-off by our opponents went clear out of the end zone, so we didn't have a chance of returning it. I had never seen any other school do that, so I now knew that these guys were real good. The first play called by our quarterback was one in which I would get the ball. He turned and handed me the ball, and before we knew it three huge linemen from the other team had hit me and driven me into the ground. As they got up, they growled and acted kind of mean. Scared to death, I ran back immediately to the huddle, where I informed the quarterback that whatever he did he definitely was not to give me the ball.

Probably being in a stupor of shock, the quarterback now called exactly the same play again. But this time as he handed me the ball, a miracle occurred—a hole appeared for me to run through. Apparently our opponents had made a mistake, but whatever the reason there was a hole. I quickly ran through it and raced for the sidelines, since many of the other team's members were pursuing me. My motive in running was not great ambition or great skill but great fear. I feared they would catch and hurt me. I continued to race towards the sideline and then cut upfield. When I stopped running I stood in our opponents' end zone, having scored a touchdown. Cheers and excitement exploded from our sideline.

This was the beginning of another miracle. Our team, once in great fear, now began to feel that we could play with those guys. We began to block, tackle, and run as never before. Not only did we do those things but also many members of our team caught the ball—an unusual feat for us. When the game ended, an amazing transformation had occurred that caused us to defeat Idaho's number 2 rated team by 20 points.

The headlines in the local paper the next morning read, "Blackfoot Upsets Highland." I choose to believe that we reached our true potential as a team. But the next weekend our school lost to a much smaller school than ours. You see, every weekend during football season some school upsets some other school's game plan. An upset causes players, coaches, fans, cheerleaders, parents, bands, and so forth to enjoy an excitement they haven't felt for some time.

Youth, you are needed in a very important game. It is your challenge to upset the adversary's game plan. You are choice spirits who have been held in reserve to come forth in this day when temptations, responsibilities, and opportunities are the very greatest. We need you to reach your full potential and play this game of life as never before.

Satan, who wanted to rob us of our agency, was cast out of our Heavenly Father's presence along with one-third of our Father's spirit children. They were cast down to this earth, where, though the scenery would change, the war would rage on. Satan's goal is to make us all miserable like himself and thus rob us of the excitement and exhilaration that truly is found in living the gospel of Jesus Christ.

What a thrill it was during this past year to receive counsel from the living prophets in the form of a booklet entitled *For the Strength of Youth*. There our priesthood leaders have shown us what the Lord would have us do in order to return to him pure and undefiled, having proven ourselves worthy of an eternity of joy in his presence. It's like having a game plan from the Lord by which to strike back at the adversary.

Let's take a look at some of the plays that the Lord would have us run against the adversary.

Music

For years I've tried to stay current with the music that teens were listening to. I've found it's impossible. As I travel from one section of the country to another I find different tastes in music, and each time I present a fireside on music, youth come up and want me to play their favorite song (which I haven't heard yet, because it isn't being played in the area where I live). Some writers have felt it best to point out the contrary life-styles of certain musicians, while others have printed the lyrics from songs that encouraged immoral activities. All this did for me, was to put things into my mind that I didn't enjoy having there.

It all came to a head on one occasion while I was attending a church dance. A song was playing that had a catchy tune, and I was enjoying dancing to it with my wife. Then a young man came up to me and said, "Brother Bird, do you know what that song is really about?" When I said no, this young man proceeded to tell me the evil meaning behind each lyric. I left the dance that night feeling confused. I had enjoyed that song until I knew what the lyrics were saying. Was it best to know what the lyrics of the song really meant, or to remain innocent, having no knowledge about the song?

I began asking myself, What is the best approach to teaching youth about music and its effects? As I pondered this, a simple statement from the First Presidency came to mind: "You cannot afford to fill your minds with unworthy music" (*For the Strength of Youth*, p. 13). They encouraged us not to listen to music that contains ideas which contradict gospel principles. This would include music that promotes Satanism or immorality, uses foul and offensive language, or in any way drives away the Spirit. What beautiful counsel from the Lord!

The prophet Mormon also gave us great counsel on how to judge music, apparel, literature, and other things the world has to offer. He said: "The Spirit of Christ is given to every man, that he may know good from evil; wherefore, I show unto you the way to judge; for every thing which inviteth to do good, and to persuade to believe in Christ, is sent forth by the power and gift of Christ; wherefore ye may know with a perfect knowledge it is of God. But whatsoever thing persuadeth men to do evil, and believe not in Christ, and deny him, and serve not God, then ye may know with a perfect knowledge it is of the devil." (Moroni 7:16-17.)

Dress and Appearance

Some time ago, while presenting a fireside to a group of youth, I invited two young people to come to the stand and respond to a question. To the young man I said: "I would like you to visit a high school in this community and bring back to this group any young woman that you perceive to be 'wild.' By *wild*, I mean one who has questionable morals, language, and feelings of self-worth. Do you think you could pick out and bring back such a person by just observing her appearance and conduct?" The same question was asked of the young woman, only I asked her to return with a young man of the same characteristics.

It was interesting to note that both of these young people said they could easily do such a thing. I then asked them to describe the appearance of the person they would bring back. The young man mentioned things like too much makeup, tight-fitting pants, wild hair, an abundance of jewelry, and so forth. The young woman said that the boy she returned with would also wear tight-fitting jeans, maybe even with holes in them. Heavy metal T-shirts, excessive jewelry, and foul language were some other traits that her returning young man would possess. It should be noted that both of these imaginary people were labeled virtually by their appearance alone. Aside from the matter of speech they could be fine individuals, but by the way they appeared they were judged to be wild. Daily our dress, grooming, and general appearance are being evaluated by those around us. We need to dress, speak, and act so that we reflect an image which enhances womanhood, magnifies manhood, and exemplifies sainthood.

"What is a modest swimsuit?" It used to be said that girls should wear a modest one-piece swimsuit and not a two-piece. But with styles changing as quickly as they do, you found that some one-piece swimsuits were far more immodest than some two-piece suits. The key word is *modest*. Girls, please take your mother or honest, best friend with you when you buy a swimsuit. Model the suit for them and seek their opinion on whether it's modest or not. Make sure it fits properly and has a good lining.

Now, to you young men. Whenever they speak to me about swimsuits, girls ask that I mention the following to all young men. Please, do not wear those "speedo bikini" swimsuits. They do not make you look "macho"—they frequently make you look sick. I'm quoting the girls now, of course. If you're involved in swimming competitions with your schools that require you to wear speedo swimsuits, be sure to wear sweats over the suits before and immediately after your event. You'll feel better, and so will those around you.

Remember, if you're not sure what's appropriate for certain occasions or activities, ask for guidelines from your parents, advisors, or bishop. They are always happy to help and are inspired to help you be the best you can be. Elder Sterling W. Sill summarized the subject of dress when he said: "A letdown in personal appearance has far more than physical significance. When ugliness gets its roots into one part of our lives, it may soon spread to every other part." (*The Quest for Excellence* [Salt Lake City: Bookcraft, 1967], p. 38.)

Media: Movies, Television, and Videocassettes

Two or three years ago my daughter went to a friend's house to view a video and have a good time. Following her return home we asked her how the evening went. She mentioned that the video being viewed downstairs was not appropriate, so she went upstairs and played a game with three others who followed her. How thrilled I was as a parent to know that one of my children was making good choices.

Now, don't get me wrong; this wasn't the first good choice one of my children had ever made. This time three others made the same wise choice and it was just exciting to have a report of youth, under negative pressure from their peers, doing what the Lord would have them do. It's interesting to have young people come and tell me what a "good" movie they have just seen. I ask what was the title of the movie and what its rating was. Sometimes they respond that it was rated R or PG-13—but that it was still good. Wanting to know more about the movie, I ask if it contained nudity, violence, or vulgarity. Once again, often the response is, "There was only one bad scene, and the language was no different than in the halls of our high school." Yet Mormon, having defined the sources of good and evil, wrote plainly and clearly, "Take heed, my beloved brethren, that ye do not judge that which is evil to be of God, or that which is good and of God to be of the devil" (Moroni 7:14).

Our Father in Heaven has counseled us as Latter-day Saints to seek after those things that are "virtuous, lovely, or of good report or praiseworthy" (Articles of Faith 1:13). Media have the great ability to give us positive experiences that can uplift, inspire, and teach moral principles. They can also make what is wrong and evil look normal, exciting, and acceptable. "In short," the First Presidency has said, "if you have any question about whether a particular movie, book, or other form of entertainment is appropriate, don't see it, don't read it, don't participate" (*For the Strength of Youth*, p. 12).

Obedience

Several years ago, when I was first hired to teach seminary, my wife and I were asked to speak in sacrament meeting in our new ward. It would be our first Sunday to meet the youth we were going to teach in this good community and their parents. At this time my wife and I were the parents of three daughters under the age of eighteen months.

My wife spoke first. While she did so, I used up everything we had brought to keep the children quiet—Cheerios, candy, and so forth. (Since this experience, I've decided it is better not to use such things in sacrament meetings.) It was now my turn to address the congregation. Partway through my talk, I noticed my wife struggling with our children. She decided to take them out of the meeting. She gently pushed the twin girls into the aisle, then turned to pick up their little baby sister, but before she could turn back around to walk out of the chapel with all three, the twin girls got loose and headed for the pulpit. Fear gripped me as they approached. They stopped first at the piano in front of the podium, where one of them began to pound on the keys. By now I was totally embarrassed, and wondering what to do. I continued to speak (or try to), as my wife, holding the baby in one arm, had now reached the piano and was herding the one twin out of the side door. Before peace and calm could return to the congregation, my second twin had found the light switches. Lights began to go off and on, and I now left the pulpit to help. My wife came back in to assist in picking up the second twin and removed her from the chapel. I returned to the pulpit and finished my talk.

Upon arriving at our trailer, my wife and I decided that if there was one thing we hoped our children would be as they grew was obedient. Our next several home evenings and discussions centered around that topic.

I've often been impressed with the thought that that's what our Father in Heaven would have us be—obedient. To follow the counsel of the Father and his Son would bring us the greatest of joy and would aid him in accomplishing his work of bringing to pass the immortality and eternal life of man (see Moses 1:39).

The War Continues

Elder Thomas S. Monson has said: "Today we are encamped against the greatest array of sin, vice, and evil ever assembled before our eyes. Such formidable enemies may cause lesser hearts to shrink or shun the fight. But the battle plan whereby we fight to save the souls of men is not our own. . . . And as we do battle against him who would thwart the purposes of God and degrade and destroy mankind, I pray that each of us will stand in his or her appointed place, that the battle for the souls of men will indeed be won; that when life's race has been run, we may hear the commendation of the Lord, 'Well done, thou good and faithful servant: thou hast been faithful over a few things, I will make thee ruler over many things: enter into the joy of the Lord.'" (*Relief Society Magazine*, April 1967, p. 247.)

This game of life must be fought as the ball game alluded to earlier in this talk was fought. We must reach our potential and defeat the opponent.

Elder Hugh B. Brown, in an address to BYU students in September 1961, said: "I come to you tonight, brothers and sisters, with a message from the President of the Church, a message which consists of two parts. First, he asked that I bring to you his love and blessing and gratitude—gratitude for the work you have done and in anticipation of the work you are going to do. The second part of his message was given to me when I asked him what I should say. He gave me two words only, and I am sure you would be glad if I would say those two words and sit down. The words were: 'Be prepared.' I hope that does not sound too ominous, but you would know it was serious if you had heard him say it."

May we truly follow the counsel of the Brethren and fight the war on this earth just as fervently as we did the War in Heaven.

Randall C. Bird, a seminary principal and teacher in Shelley, Idaho, has served as a track and football coach and has been listed in Who's Who in America. *He likes fishing, sports, collecting sports cards and memorabilia, and reading. In high school he was named to the Idaho all-state teams in football and track. Randall and his wife, Carla, have six children.*

CHAPTER 16

It Was Only a Quarter-Inch but Everyone Noticed

Jill S. Cloward

Several years ago I decided to make my daughters some teddy bears for Christmas, and I wanted them to be just perfect. I looked in all the toy stores at the ready-made bears, and then I selected the "perfect" pattern and fabric. I hurried home, carefully cut out the bears, and began sewing.

I had done quite a bit of sewing and knew that most patterns call for a 5/8" seam. So I stitched the first half of the bear in 5/8", before realizing that this pattern called for a 3/8" seam. I was not about to unpick that bear! I figured that it was only a quarter-inch different and probably it wouldn't matter that much, so I stitched the other half with a 3/8" seam.

After stuffing the bear I sat him on the counter so I could admire my work. He was definitely lopsided! No matter how much I pushed and pulled on him, he remained lopsided. I rationalized that it wasn't that obvious, and I decided to wait and see if anyone else noticed how lopsided he was.

When my mother stopped by the next morning, I carefully produced the bear from his secret Christmas hiding place and sat him on the counter for her admiration. She didn't disappoint me. She said, "Oh! He is so cute! I love this fabric, and it will match their room perfectly! Where did you ever find the pattern? But, Jill, there's just one thing—did you notice—he's lopsided?"

Well, I knew that if my mother noticed, everyone else would too. So I unpicked the back seam and removed all of the stuffing. Then I turned the bear inside-out, unpicked all of the 5/8" seams, and re-stitched them with 3/8" seams. Then I turned the bear right-side out and stuffed him again. Finally, when I placed him on the counter, he sat there true and even, just the way he should have in the first place.

From that experience I learned an important lesson about sewing. That is, that even a seam as small and insignificant as a quarter-inch can make a big difference in how my bear turned out, or how a garment can fit.

It is the same way in our lives. The little thoughts, the little feelings, the little attitudes, and the little quarter-inch decisions will make all the difference in who we become and how our lives turn out.

One of my favorite stories in the Old Testament is the story of Joseph, who was sold into Egypt by his brothers. He was the eleventh of twelve sons. His brothers became so jealous of him that they sold him as a slave. However, I like to think that when they were young, Joseph and his brothers had some good times together. Let me illustrate with an experience in my own family.

When my oldest son, Aaron, was in high school, he was pretty *cool*. In fact, he was *way cool*. He was so cool that if you didn't believe me you could have just asked him. He would have told you how cool he was. As a freshman in high school he lettered in basketball. As a sophomore, a junior, and a senior, he was on the starting line-up of the varsity team, and he played in the state tournament games, where all four years the team placed. As a senior he was also the studentbody president at Spanish Fork High School. He became so cool in his senior year that we didn't even need air conditioning in our home. He would just walk into the room, and everyone would chill out!

After basketball practice Aaron would come in the back door, slam his books on the counter, and drop his gym bag onto the floor. He would open the fridge, chug down a gallon of milk, and then grab a box of Oreo Cookies and a bag of Dorito Corn Chips and sit in the blue chair in our family room. He was so cool that he could watch ten television programs at the same time. All he had to do was move his finger from one button to another on the remote controller.

As soon as he was comfortable and settled, his younger brother, Ben, would sneak into the room. Ben, who was nine years old at the time, idolized Aaron and did anything he could to get his attention. He usually made loud, obnoxious noises, and threw spitwads or elastic bands. Finally he would hit Aaron and then run for dear life, yelling, "Touched you last!"

Aaron would reply in a low monotone, "Leave me alone."

Again, Ben would sneak in and repeat the action, yelling, "Ha! Ha! Touched you last!"

Aaron's voice would become menacing. "I said, leave me alone!"

"Ha! Ha! Ha! Touched you last!"

"I said, leave me alone, or I'm gonna kill ya!"

That was usually the ultimate challenge for Ben, and he would come into the room one more time, taunting, "Ha! Ha! you can't get me, big ears! Touched you last!"

At this, Aaron would lunge from the blue chair, grab Ben, throw him down on the floor, and sit on him, where he would proceed to do the "tortures."

First, he did the turkey torture. It was a simple torture; he thumped on Ben's chest while Ben hollered the Tarzan yell.

The second torture was the tickle torture. Aaron tickled Ben unmercifully, saying, "Laugh if you like it. Ha! Ha! Laugh if you like it! Oh! You're laughing, you must like it!"

As the tortures escalated, both boys would be laughing uncontrollably, and soon Ben would be crying. At that point Aaron would do the ultimate and final torture. He would place all of his weight on Ben and say, "You're hot."

Ben would say "I'm hot. I'm hot!"

Then Aaron would say slowly and methodically, "You're hot, and you can't breathe."

Ben would choke, "I can't breathe. I can't breathe!"

Aaron would quietly whisper, "You're hot. You can't breathe, and you're gonna *die*!"

Ben would gasp, "I'm dying! I'm dying! I can't brea.t.h.e!"

Finally, Aaron would ask, "Do you promise you'll leave me alone?"

"Yes, I promise. I pro.m.i.s.e!" Ben would croak in a whisper.

So Aaron would let him go and would sit back down in the blue chair to watch television with his Oreo Cookies and Dorito Corn Chips.

Within five minutes Ben would run back in, tears still in his eyes, and yell angrily, "Touched you last, big ears!" And the whole thing would start all over again.

I like to think that in the beginning Joseph and his brothers had that same kind of relationship, and that they played the same kind of games that brothers play; that they wrestled, and tickled, and generally horsed around.

But as time went on, some of the brothers began to be a little bit jealous of Joseph. They noticed that their father favored Joseph; and Joseph's telling them his prophetic dreams didn't help the relationship. So they let their jealous feelings grow until they became lopsided in their feelings toward Joseph. Ultimately they became so lopsided in their jealousy that one day, as they saw him approaching, some of them decided to kill him.

The oldest brother, Reuben, perhaps remembering earlier, happy times they had shared, persuaded the others not to kill him. He suggested that instead they put him in a deep hole they had seen in the wilderness, and this they did.

Later another brother, Judah, also fearing for Joseph's life, suggested that they sell Joseph to a group of Ishmaelite merchants who were journeying to Egypt. They sold their brother for twenty pieces of silver.

Can you imagine the sense of betrayal Joseph must have felt? Can you think of his fear? his anger? his deep sorrow? Can you comprehend his awful humiliation?

Joseph was taken to Egypt by strangers, where he was sold again, as a slave to Potiphar. There he worked hard until he became an overseer in Potiphar's house.

After a time, Potiphar's wife "cast her eyes upon Joseph; and she said, Lie with me" (Genesis 39:7). Joseph repeatedly refused her advances and tried to avoid being near her. One day, when she found him alone in the house, she approached him again, but he fled out of the house, leaving his cloak in her hands. She became so angry that she lied to her husband and accused Joseph falsely. Potiphar believed his wife, and Joseph was cast into prison.

He remained true and faithful to Heavenly Father, yet he was cast into prison. Can you imagine how he must have felt then? I am sure there were days when Joseph must have asked, "Heavenly Father, where are you? Do you still love me? What have I done to deserve this?"

Each of us have times in our own lives when we think those same kinds of wondering thoughts. We have challenges that cause us to ask: "Heavenly Father, why me? This is too hard. This is not fair."

As you know, Joseph refused to allow those little thoughts and feelings to become lopsided. Instead of seeking revenge and trying to get even with his brothers, he remained faithful to our Father and thereby was later able to save his family from famine.

By the time his brothers came to Egypt searching for food, Pharaoh had given Joseph responsibility over all the storehouses in Egypt. They approached him, wanting to buy food. We read about the test he gave them, and then his ultimate response to them: "And he fell upon his brother Benjamin's neck, and wept; and Benjamin wept upon his neck. Moreover he kissed all his brethren, and wept upon them." (Genesis 45:14-15.)

Remember that the little thoughts, the little feelings, the little attitudes, and the little quarter-inch decisions will make all the difference in our lives.

I want to tell you a story about a girl I will call Susan. I have known her and her family since she was born, and have watched her mature into a beautiful young woman.

After Susan graduated from high school she moved away from home to attend college. Her parents weren't able to provide for all of the financial expenses of college, so it became necessary for Susan to obtain employment. She was successful in her effort, but the only problem was that her job required her to work on Sundays. She felt that this wasn't too critical, since some organizations—hospitals, for example—must remain open on Sundays. Susan continued to attend her church meetings in the mornings, and then went to work on Sunday afternoons. After a few months she began to feel that she was too restricted by church attendance, and she started missing a few of her meetings.

One evening after work, some of Susan's new acquaintances invited her to go to the city and dance with them. She was excited at this, because she was a good dancer and enjoyed dancing. The only problem was that the dancing was in a bar. Susan was a little concerned, but she rationalized that she was only going there to dance and didn't plan to drink or smoke. Although the music was a little more hard rock than she usually listened to, she continued to go dancing with her friends in the bar.

One night her friends invited her to go to the local coffee

shop after the dance, in order to unwind. Although she didn't smoke, or drink coffee, she went with them and visited until 2:00 A.M. These activities continued for several weeks, and she began to meet a whole new group of friends.

One night one of the guys she had met invited her to a party the following weekend, and she accepted the invitation. At the party a spiked punch bowl was served. Susan had never drunk alcohol before. Anxious to be accepted by her new friends, she decided that it wouldn't hurt to try it once, just to see what it was like. She was invited to several more parties with her new friends, and she continued to participate in these new activities.

After a few weeks one of the guys asked if he could drive her home from a party. She agreed, and on the way home they parked for a while, because "I never get to see you alone, and I just want to talk." They talked until late into the night. This activity continued for a few months, until they were doing much more than "just talking."

Finally, one day Susan discovered she was pregnant. Overnight her decisions had changed from, "What am I going to wear to the dance Friday night?" to, "What am I going to do with this baby, and how am I going to tell my parents?"

I watched as Susan struggled through this agonizing time of her life, and as she tried to make decisions about her baby and their future. Susan never considered an abortion. Marriage was not an alternative for her, because when the baby's father found out she was pregnant he moved to California in the middle of the night. He never told his mother or father about the baby or Susan. For her, there were two alternatives. She could have the baby and raise it as a single parent or she could place the baby for adoption.

I wish that each of you could have seen, as I did, the heartache and sorrow Susan experienced. I wish you could have seen the anguish of her mother and father and her brothers and sisters. I wish you could have seen the confusion and disappointment of her nieces and nephews.

And finally, I wish you could have been there as Susan tearfully related to me how she dressed her new baby daughter in a little pink dress. She put a tiny pink bow in her hair and then took pictures with a whole roll of film. Then she tenderly wrapped her in a soft white blanket and held her, and loved her, for the last time on this earth, before gently handing her to the social worker for placement.

Does it matter if you work on Sundays? Does it matter if you go to a bar just to dance and listen to the music? Does it matter if you stay out until one and two in the morning? Does it matter if you try a spiked punch bowl, just once, to see what it's like? Does it matter if you park on a dark road "just to talk"?

Does it matter? Ask Susan.

The little thoughts, the little feelings, the little attitudes, and the little quarter-inch decisions will make all the difference in your lives.

Mormon tells us: "Every thing which inviteth to do good, and to persuade to believe in Christ, is sent forth by the power and gift of Christ. . . . But whatsoever thing persuadeth men to do evil, and believe not in Christ, and deny him, and serve not God, then ye may know with a perfect knowledge it is of the devil . . . for he persuadeth no man to do good, no not one." (Moroni 7:16-17.)

It is my fervent hope and prayer that you will choose to follow your good thoughts; that you will allow only the good feelings and attitudes to remain in your heart; and finally, that you will always remember that the little quarter-inch decisions will determine your destiny.

Jill S. Cloward lives in Salem, Utah, and defines her occupation as a "domestic engineer (housewife)." She likes to spend time traveling, snorkeling, cooking, and sewing and says that shopping is her favorite form of relaxation. Jill admires the "I can do anything" attitude of youth and finds that working with young people is always an adventure. She and her husband, David, are the parents of four children.

CHAPTER 17

Some Miracles Take Time

Art E. Berg

The sound of breaking glass and twisting metal broke the cold, silent December air. The world was in a violent spin. Control was gone from me as the forces of nature and physics wreaked their own lessons of havoc and destruction. Suddenly I was free. Free, that is, until my body landed in a heap on the frozen desert floor. My world went black.

Only ten short hours earlier, Christmas Day, my whole world had revolved on an axis of happiness, pleasure, and personal enrichment. I had no idea how quickly it could all change—pleasure be replaced by pain, happiness become misery, and enrichment evolve into a battle of survival.

For most others in California, this Christmas was to be like any other. The nights were crisp and cool, and the dark skies were filled with the brilliance and glow of the stars that seemed to be made just for me. They were nights made for romance and love. This Christmas was special. For me, it wasn't so much the day that mattered as it was the time of year. I had a lot of things to think about.

Taken from the talk tape and book *Some Miracles Take Time*, by Art Berg, produced and published by Covenant Communications, Inc.

I had been home from my mission for one year. I was filled with the success experiences returning missionaries like to tell about. The Lord had been good to me. I felt very blessed. I also felt I was doing my part, doing the things I knew would make my Father in Heaven pleased with me. The Church and the gospel were the very center of my life. I enjoyed visits to the temple, moments of solemn, heart-felt prayer, and daily feasts from the scriptures. I felt a longing to draw nearer to my God and was acting on it.

Activity, love, excitement—each filled the reservoirs of my days. I was active physically; I was a competitive water-skier; I snow-skied, played golf, tennis, racquetball, basketball; bowled on a league; and ran nearly every day. I had just started a new tennis court construction company, so my financial future looked rewarding and bright. But most important, I was in love with the most beautiful girl in the world. Tonight, I was driving to be with her and to finish the plans for our wedding, which was to take place in five short weeks.

Little did I know how much my life would change after that night.

Leaving for Utah that Christmas night seemed no different from all the times I had done it before. Through the years I had made the trip dozens of times with friends and family. It was no big deal. We had a family prayer before I left, as we always did. Kneeling in a formation which never quite resembled a "family circle," we prayed for the usual things you would pray for before such a trip—a safe journey, the Spirit to guide my actions, that God would keep and protect me until I arrived at my destination.

I was travelling with John, a new friend of mine. We drove away at about seven o'clock that Christmas evening.

I drove for the first eight hours of the trip, mostly through California and into Nevada. By then my eyes felt heavy, and I was ready for some sleep. It was John's turn at the wheel; he had been resting for some time now. I comfortably arranged myself in the reclined passenger seat, fastened my seat belt, and quickly dozed off as John drove us away into the night.

What seemed only minutes later (but was actually more than an hour and a half) I was suddenly awakened as I felt the car swerve to the left. John had fallen asleep at the wheel, had lost control of the car, and it was heading for a cement divider along the right side of the highway. "Hold on," John yelled, and I heard the frightened desperation in his voice. Trying to avoid the wall, he pulled hard to the left on the wheel. But it was too late. The car, traveling at freeway speed, hit the cement embankment. The tires rode the embankment to the top, hurtling the car over it. The car, a little Volkswagen Rabbit, rolled down the side of the road, each rotation strewing pieces of metal and glass along the way, until it came to a stop in an unrecognizable form. John, with his white-knuckled hands still clinging to the steering wheel, immediately looked to see if I was all right. His heart stopped: I was gone!

John quickly pulled himself from the tangled mass. His voice rang out in the clear night. "Art! Art!" Listening intently, he heard only the quiet sounds of a gentle wind whispering back. Fear washed over him in a wave of terror. "Art!" he yelled again, now running blindly in the darkness and stumbling on the rough terrain. No answer. Finally, on hands and knees, John groped through the thick darkness, feeling his way along, calling my name again and again. After what seemed an eternity in a dark world, he heard soft groans of pain and rushed to my side.

When I regained consciousness I was lying on the floor of the Nevada desert. I didn't have much idea of what was happening, but I knew I wasn't dead yet, because I was hurting too much.

My face was badly scraped and bloody, and my lips were torn and cracked. I gasped for short breaths of air as the blood warmed my face. Fortunately, I did not know then what had really happened. I had done the unthinkable; I had broken my neck, and now I was passing in and out between reality and unconsciousness. I had always thought that when a person broke his neck, he died. It was that simple in my mind. All I knew was that something was seriously wrong.

When I seemed somewhat coherent, John asked me how I was doing. I told him things were not right. I told him I could not feel my legs. I asked him if he would give me a priesthood blessing and promise me that my legs would be all right—that I'd be all right. He said he didn't know if he could do that. I pleaded with him to ask the Lord if he could. Humbly, anxiously, John knelt beside his hurting friend and petitioned God to open the windows of heaven and bless his frightened children.

The air seemed still and calm as two priesthood bearers approached their Lord in prayer. A dark, cold desert became a temple where God and men became peacefully close. With the power of great rushing winds, yet with the whisper of a still, small voice,

God gave his approval for such a blessing. John, now with deep confidence, laid his hands upon my head and pronounced the blessing in the healing name of Jesus Christ. He blessed me that my legs would be all right—that I would recover completely and be healed. That was all I needed to hear. The salt from my tears stung my wounded face, and I sank back into unconsciousness.

Minutes following the accident, truck drivers saw the twisted wreckage and radioed for emergency help. Because the accident occurred some forty miles east of Las Vegas, it was nearly an hour before an ambulance could arrive on the scene. In the meantime, John took his leather jacket off and placed it across my broken body to keep me warm until help arrived. Even today, his blood-stained coat reminds him of that fateful night.

My eyes opened slowly and painfully as I looked up into the bright lights of the emergency room. A doctor was standing over me stitching my forehead, lips, and nose. It was hard for me to see. I later learned that one of my eyes was filled with blood and was swollen beyond recognition. I heard muffled voices, none that I could distinguish. A prayer left my lips—"God, please help me"—and I was gone again.

Later, I was pronounced by my doctors as being a quadriplegic, having been paralyzed from the chest down. I lost the use of my feet and legs. I lost the use of my stomach muscles, two out of my three major chest muscles, my right tricep, most of the strength in my arms and shoulders, and the complete use of my hands. The doctors, through a series of discussions, told me that my life would never be the same again. They told me to dream new dreams and think new thoughts. They made it clear that, aside from being confined to a wheelchair for the rest of my life, I would never work again, because ninety-three percent of those in my condition never do. They said that I would never drive again; that for the rest of my life I would be dependent upon family and friends to eat, to get dressed, and to get from place to place. They said I would never get married, because who would want me anyway? And they told me that I would never again be able to participate in any type of athletic activity or competitive event. For the first time in my young life, I was really afraid. I was afraid that what they said might really be true.

I cried myself to sleep that night, as I did many nights. I cried because of physical pain and discomfort. I cried because others suffered with me. But most of all, I cried for all the dreams I had ever cherished which would never be fulfilled. Hope is born of dreams, and where were my dreams now? I had hit the bottom.

Years later, as I write these words, tears come to my eyes as I consider the blessing the Lord granted me that night. Some wonder, however, what became of that grand and marvelous blessing. If you were here with me today you would see me sitting before you in a wheelchair, still crippled from a devastating accident. My hands are chapped, rough, and dry from years of pushing myself from place to place; my paralyzed fingers are curled and stiff from disuse. My legs are thin and wiry from sitting for so long, and I am sometimes struck down with high, uncontrollable fevers that last for days without relief. Seeing me, you might ask, "Why?" Why, if the promise of recovery was declared, should I still be suffering today? Why—if the Lord's priesthood had the power and authority to heal, to deliver from pain, misery, and struggle—why should I be denied that blessing after years of waiting?

The power of the priesthood is real. I know that God lives and that he loves his children. His glorious ways are not our ways and are not always clear. While we do not know and understand all things, there are some things we do know. Some designs *are* clear. Some truths have been revealed which bring meaning to the seemingly meaningless. God is not dead, nor is his priesthood power. They function today as in the meridian of time, even as when our Savior walked among mortal men. I know, as sure as I am alive, that when I have done all I need to do while in this wheelchair, when I have accomplished all God intends for me to accomplish in this condition, when I have learned the things I need to learn—when all this is done God *will* open the windows of heaven and make his promises efficacious in my life. I will most assuredly walk again in some future mortal day. For some this is hard to understand; for me, it is a reality. God has spoken these truths to my heart.

While I live each day with the promise of a brighter future, some have wondered why such a tragedy was necessary. The miracle of a moment could have stemmed the suffering, pain, and anguish of long years. Why would such a miracle be delayed? Is there purpose in waiting? All my life I believed that the power and miracles of the Lord's priesthood produced instantaneous results. With my body suffering the effects of my accident, I was prepared to learn one of the most significant—albeit forgotten—ingredients of miracles: time itself.

In our modern age of technology, complete with jet propulsion, automobiles, space shuttles, computers, and fax machines, information and people race from one end of our world to the other at inconceivable speeds. In a day when *tomorrow* is interpreted as "too late," and *now* has become the operative word in business, the concept of time has taken on a whole new meaning.

We live in an "instant" world; a world where if you cannot have it now, do it now, or enjoy it now, it is esteemed as being of little value. In the Church this often translates into the perception that a miracle must always happen "instantaneously" in order to be regarded as a miracle. That is not so. The miracle that some have called time many fail to recognize as such. Yet the greatest blessings have come into my own life only after long effort, hard work, priesthood power, and time.

President Spencer W. Kimball has said there are "infinitely more miracles today than in any age past, and just as wondrous." Then where are they, and why do you and I seem to miss them? Where are those instantaneous miracles of yesteryears? But, were they instantaneous? And are they only reserved for days gone past?

While I was speaking at a youth conference in Louisiana, a young man asked me a very pointed but honest question. "What is a miracle?" He asked innocently, but with the deep desire to truly know. While varying in power and display, miracles are those events or developments which we could not bring about by our own strength or resources but which require the direct intervention of the power and priesthood of God. That would include the restoring of sight to a blind man, parting the waters of the Red Sea, taking the hate and venom from the heart of a mother whose husband has been brutally murdered in cold blood, or enabling a weak and paralyzed quadriplegic to stretch beyond the limited bounds of ability to the realization of his otherwise unattainable dreams. All required the mercy and power of a loving Father and a compassionate Savior. The sun's "standing still" for a day at Joshua's command is no more significant an event than a retarded child's learning to write if both accomplishments were beyond the natural reach of the individual. Miracles are accomplished by the Lord's omnipotent power coupled with human efforts and faith.

As we walk along the dusty streets of ancient Jerusalem through the words and images of the scriptures, we read that as Jesus and his disciples passed by the temple walls they came upon a man who had been blind from birth. For years he had come there, perhaps hoping that a deliverer, such as Elisha, would one day come. And so each day he waited.

As Jesus passed by, the disciples asked, "Master, who did sin, this man, or his parents, that he was born blind?" With infinite knowledge he responded, "Neither has this man sinned, nor his parents: but that the works of God should be made manifest in him." Using the moisture from his own spittle, he formed from the dust of the earth clay, with which he anointed the blind man's eyes. In a voice filled with compassion and foresight he commanded the man, "Go, wash in the pool of Siloam." (See John 9:1-7.)

As quickly as any blind man can make his way through the obstacles and crowds of a bustling marketplace, he made his way to the pool. Cupping his hands together, he gathered the healing water to his face. As the water fell, his eyes were flooded with light. Eyes once shut with darkness now had a new view of the world. What a miracle! Who could not sense in some limited form the significant blessing which had come into this simple man's life! Surely, he would never be the same again.

I don't know how old the blind man was, but was the miracle of his life just an "instant" thing? Was it the miracle of a day, or an hour, or even a moment? Or was it the concluding event of a miracle that took a lifetime? Through the vision of our own finite perspective, do we look upon the one act as though it stood alone, independent of a lifetime of hopes, prayers, growth, faith, and miracles?

How many of us have read about the splendor of the Lord's miracles in both the Old and the New World and have ached to feel the power of his healing touch in our own lives? Even today there are those who are blind or lame or diseased, and whose hearts and lips have extended toward the heavens in question and desire, seeking the power of the Savior's healing touch. And then there are those who live with broken hearts and homes, discouragement and rejection, frustration and misery, and who struggle daily to find meaning and hope. Each seeks the healing touch. Each wonders how to obtain the power of the Master for that purpose. Some still hope for the light, while others see only darkness.

Regardless of the circumstances or struggle, each battles against a common enemy—time. Minutes pass slowly and days seem to extend forever when we struggle under the burdens of suffering, adversity, or pain. Time becomes the adversary, reluctant to release us from its grasp. As the minutes blend into hours, the hours into days, and the days into years, the purpose and meaning of it all becomes vague and distorted.

Yet perhaps the greatest miracle of all is that you and I can change and grow while we sojourn in this mortal probation. The miracle of change and growth has been reserved for mankind and his eternal offspring alone. No other of God's creatures, large or small, can make this glorious claim.

Without time and experience the process of change and growth would become frustrated and impossible. If every blessing bestowed, every healing delivered, and every righteous exercising of the Lord's priesthood produced "instantaneous" results, we would be robbed of the fundamental element of time and thus would be denied the greatest miracle of all, the transformation of our hearts, minds, souls, characters. How many years and months the blind man suffered we do not know. But which was the greater miracle, the opening of his darkened eyes or the myriad opportunities for change and growth which were given him only through those years of waiting?

If our lives were left absent of struggle, suffering, adversity, pain, and anguish, would healing miracles exist at all? And if, in the finality of life, we pass beyond, having never personally witnessed the majesty and power of the Lord's mighty arm as it is revealed in some of our darkest hours, then a tragedy truly has occurred.

My story, like yours, is about miracles. It is about the "works of God being made manifest" in our daily lives. It's not just about stupendous or earth-shattering events, but about the small private moments in which the Lord reveals his mighty arm. In the equation of priesthood, miracles, and infinite power, some of us have forgotten the critical and often essential ingredient called time. What we sometimes call our enemy, miracles have paradoxically embraced as friend. "Therefore, dearly beloved brethren, let us cheerfully do all things that lie in our power; and then may we stand still, and with the utmost assurance, to see the salvation of God, and for his arm to be revealed" (D&C 123:17).

Eight years ago, while lying in a hospital bed with the sacred words of a priesthood blessing still echoing in my ears, I wondered when my miracle would come. How much time? But time was all I had. And so I began to relearn—like a child—how to do everything in my life. I remember spending hour after hour stacking little blocks on top of one another, trying to learn how to use my hands again the way they now were. It wouldn't have been so bad either if the little blocks didn't have ducks and lambs on the side of them, and the letters A, B, and C.

One morning I sat in front of my breakfast and looked at my new challenge. One of the many things I had to relearn as a quadriplegic was how to eat breakfast. I know that eating breakfast doesn't sound like that hard a task. Well, the food wasn't my problem; it was getting the food to my mouth successfully that was the challenge. My hands were paralyzed, so I had to use a special instrument to help me pick up my fork and raise it to my mouth. To complicate matters, I was required to wear a chest strap to keep me from falling out of my chair. Wearing my steel halo brace caused me to be extremely top heavy. Without the use of my stomach muscles to help keep me upright and with no use of my neck and head to assist in balancing me, I was strapped in for my own safety.

I had two requests of my therapist that morning. The first was that I wanted to eat breakfast by myself. She agreed to give me thirty minutes. My second request took her even more by surprise. Tired of wearing a restraining belt around my chest wherever I went, I was anxious to try life without it. The therapist responded, "Are you absolutely sure?" Smiling, I calmly assured her of my desire. Hesitantly, she unfastened the strap and left.

I vividly remember what I was going to eat that morning. It was scrambled eggs with a hot biscuit. Reaching for the fork, I maneuvered it between my fingers to try to get some kind of a hold on it. Once it felt reasonably secure, I lifted it toward the plate. With my arm extended directly in front of me I was presented with a balance problem I had not anticipated. Even though my sense of equilibrium was not completely accurate, I recognized from the sight of the fast-approaching plate of food that I was falling forward. Since I had little use of my weak arms, any attempt to stop myself was futile. With the weight of the halo brace pushing me forward, my face landed squarely in my plate of food.

I listened for a moment to see if I could hear anyone. Then, using my weakened arms, I tried to sit myself up again. That option was out. I was stuck right there, face down in my scrambled eggs. Now, with a whole new perspective on the four basic food groups, two thoughts crossed my mind. The first was that this was probably going to be one of the longest twenty-eight minutes of my life. The second thought was that I probably wouldn't get into a more advantageous position for eating for a long time . . . so I ate my breakfast. Since then I've never had the same appreciation for scrambled eggs and biscuits!

At the time we had agreed upon the therapist walked back into the room and, seeing my situation, quickly rushed to my side and pulled me out of my plate. I showed obvious relief to have my vision of the room restored. The therapist, noticing that the plate was shiny and clean, excitedly asked me, "Well, how did you do?" "All right," I responded. "It was a little tough getting the butter on the biscuit . . . but I did all right!"

Shortly thereafter the doctors took me into a separate room and explained to me that there were different terrains in life—hills, concrete, gravel, carpeting. They told me that because of the strength needed to push a manual wheelchair—strength which I would never have—in order to get around at all in life I would need an electric wheelchair. But I had a fear of the electric wheelchair. I feared that if I got used to the ease and convenience of just pushing a button to attain what I desired my strength, enthusiasm, and self-esteem would slowly deteriorate.

Now came the problem of convincing the staff what I felt was best for me. When I first mentioned my feelings they resisted strongly, concerned for my new future. "You must use an electric wheelchair, Art. To get around this hospital on smooth linoleum floors is one thing, but for you to challenge the world without the use of a motor is not feasible. You'll need an electric chair."

"You don't understand," I replied. "I do not want an electric wheelchair. I won't use it. I want a manual chair."

Finally they consented to consider my proposal if I could pass a test of my strength and ability. On the first floor of the hospital a track had been laid out measuring one-eighth of a mile. If I could push that distance in less than thirty minutes, I could have my manual wheelchair.

The morning of the event arrived. Doctors and nurses all stood around—anxious to see if I could finish—with a stopwatch to mark my progress. A piece of tape was stretched across the floor in front of me to signify the starting and finish line. Finally they clicked the watch and said, "Go!"

The first hallway was relatively easy as I made my way slowly down toward the end. By the time I reached the end of that first hallway, however, I was wondering whether I had made a wrong turn; my arms and shoulders began to tire and I began to question whether I would finish. In a state of exhaustion I made my way down the second hallway, the third, and finally the last, then crossed over that finish line—all in exactly twenty-eight minutes. So I got my manual wheelchair.

It wasn't long after that when I had cause to wonder whether my decision was wise. It was that time of the year when I needed to go shopping by myself, so I went to Eastridge Mall, a shopping center in San Jose, California. It's three stories high and has one hundred and ninety-six stores—a shopper's dream. I was on the third level and needed to get back to the second, so I waited by the elevator doors. As those doors opened and closed I watched as young mothers and their children in strollers crowded on and off, on and off. I knew then that if I was going to successfully exceed the credit limit on my Visa card, I would need to find an alternate route.

Now, if you can, visualize with me for a moment. The mall has long, sloping ramps that extend from one level of the mall down to the next. As I sat at the top of that great abyss and looked down into the valley below, I was so sure—so confident—that I could manage that kind of descent that I waited for everyone else to get off the ramp. Then I pushed off! When I did so I noticed an interesting thing—I accelerated! I began to go faster and faster down the ramp. Not having the full use of my hands, in an attempt to slow down I had to use my palms to put outside pressure on the ring. No matter how hard I pushed, however, I continued to go faster and faster.

It was about that time too that I began to smell burning flesh coming from my hands, and then I knew I was in trouble. Being the good Boy Scout that I was, I obviously became more concerned for the safety of the young mothers and children at the *bottom* of the ramp than I was for myself—I mean, after all, what more injury can you do to a quadriplegic? I figured that maybe I'd even *fix* something! So I began to wave my arms in the air, yelling, "Get out of the way! Get out of the way!" Mothers ran to the right and children ran to the left.

I noticed that an interesting thing happened when I waved my arms about—I accelerated! Well, I hit the bottom of that ramp at full speed. I don't know how fast I was going . . . eighty . . . ninety miles per hour! (At least it felt like it!)

I raced right down through the middle of all those good folks as fast as I could go. Right in front of me was a store. I shot into that store and tore down the middle of it as I continued to wave my arms and shout, "Get out of the way!" Salesmen jumped over counters, and customers hid behind pedestals. But the person who really looked worried was the man in the very back, behind the repair counter. His eyes were about as big as saucers, and getting bigger.

Well, I am a lucky man. There was carpeting on the floor, with thick padding underneath. I began to slow down, and I finally came to a stop—right in front of the repair counter.

When I went back to the hospital about a year and a half after I had left it, I decided to try that indoor track just one more time—the one that had previously taken twenty-eight minutes. This time there was nobody there except me—no doctors, nurses, or therapists, not even Dallas to encourage me. The tape was still on the floor, cracked and yellowing. Using the second hand on my watch to time me, I took off. In exactly one minute and fifty-eight seconds later I crossed that line again! Tears rolled down my cheeks as I reflected back over the months and years of effort, prayers, faith, and struggle which had been expended to reach this simple point in time and experience. I could not have felt more happy. Some people would not call that a miracle, but I do. And for the first time in my life I learned that dreams are never destroyed by circumstances. Dreams are born in the heart and in the mind, and only there can they ever die.

I returned to my tennis court construction company and ran it for another two years before selling it. Afterwards I sold computers for a national sales firm for three and a half years, during which time I received three national sales awards for my efforts. Why? Not because I am a great salesman, but because the power of the priesthood is real—because miracles happen today to you and to me. For the last three years I have owned and operated three bookstores in the Salt Lake City area—a dream come true for me.

I have learned how to drive again. I am completely independent and able to take care of myself. I go where I want to go and do what I want to do. Since that day of the accident more than seven years ago, eighty percent of the feeling has returned to my body—the first major step on a long road to complete recovery. I also married that same beautiful and wonderful girl a year and a half after that fateful day.

I have also returned to the world of sports. I have learned how to swim—just like a rock! I have learned how to play tennis and rugby, to snow-ski and scuba dive, and even to parasail—to my knowledge, I am the first quadriplegic of record to parasail. I also compete in wheelchair racing, finishing a twenty-six-mile marathon in less than three hours. For the past two years I have been training for a race which will be held in Alaska called the Race of the Midnight Sun—it's the world's longest wheelchair marathon. It is three hundred and sixty miles long and will take nine days to complete. Some miracles really do take time.

It is my testimony that God truly lives. I know that he loves you and that he loves me. Sometimes, while you and I struggle under the pain, frustration, discouragement, loneliness, and tragedies of this life, we cry out and wish that someone would take it all away. I know that our Father in Heaven can do that—but I also know that he loves you and me more than that and so sometimes he blesses you and me with a miracle called time. Oh, I believe in miracles, I really do. However, I also know that *some* miracles just take time.

And thank God for that.

Art E. Berg owns and operates three bookstores in the Salt Lake area. A professional motivational speaker to church and youth groups, he is also the author of a book entitled Some Miracles Take Time. *He enjoys wheelchair racing, boating, parasailing, and traveling. Art is an Eagle Scout and has worked with youth as a Sunday School teacher, a seminary teacher, and a teachers quorum advisor. He is married to Dallas Howard Berg, Utah's 1981 Junior Miss.*

CHAPTER 18

Mending the Broken Heart

Curtis Galke

Teachers in medical school did their best to prepare me for hospital work, but even with all I had learned from them I wasn't prepared for what happened to me late one February evening. I was "on call" that evening, which meant I was to spend the night in the hospital to take care of any medical problems that might arise. It was almost one o'clock in the morning, most of my work had been done, and I was determined to get at least a couple of hours' sleep. When my pager went off, calling me to the emergency room, I suspected it would be a sleepless night.

I ran quickly through the quiet, sterile halls, wondering what would be waiting for me. When I arrived, I was informed that several teenagers had been in a knife fight and were only three minutes away from our hospital by ambulance. We hurriedly prepared the trauma rooms. I continued to wonder who they were, what could have happened, and how badly were they injured.

I didn't have long to wonder, as the large automatic doors soon swung open and two stretchers raced toward us. I looked down at the young man to whom I had been assigned. All I knew was his first name. Juan appeared to be about fifteen years old. I quickly looked him over while the nurses and other students hooked him up to several monitors.

At first glance Juan's condition looked pretty good. There were plenty of scrapes and bruises, but I noticed only two or three stab wounds that would need to be closed. The intense feeling in the room let up considerably as we came to accept that Juan wasn't too badly hurt. I tried to strike up a conversation with him as I began to stitch up some of his larger wounds. I found out that the fight had started over a girl and had escalated from there. But as Juan continued to speak to me I noticed that his speech became more slurred, until he suddenly lost consciousness. The nurses were shouting that his pulse had dropped and he was having dangerous changes in his blood pressure. As a third-year medical student, I soon realized that I was in over my head. The supervising emergency-room doctor noticed that I needed some help and ran over to look at Juan. He found a small puncture wound on the left side of the patient's chest. Putting all of the symptoms together, the doctor concluded that this puncture wound must have penetrated Juan's heart and that he was bleeding from that hole in his heart.

The doctor moved quickly. Making sure Juan was adequately sedated, he took a scalpel and made an incision from the breast bone around to his back, explaining that Juan would only survive for a matter of minutes unless we plugged the hole in his heart. With the incision made, the doctor spread Juan's ribs apart and asked me to reach into his chest and pull his heart to the surface so we could examine it. (No one had told me there would be nights like this!) I did what I was asked to do and slowly brought Juan's heart out to where we could all see it. I couldn't believe it! I actually had Juan's heart beating in my hand, whereas only minutes earlier he and I had been talking with each other.

We looked closely and found the hole in his heart. The doctor told me to put my index finger in the hole to stop the bleeding, and although it didn't sound like the most scientific thing to do, I didn't argue. I jumped onto the stretcher with my finger still in Juan's heart and rode to the operating room, where a heart surgeon was ready to repair the hole.

I'm told that most people don't survive experiences like that. Juan did. Hours later in the intensive care unit, he began to wake up. I was eager to talk with him. I imagined his first words would be "Gee, thanks," or "My chest hurts!" Instead he asked me, "Do you know whether or not I was able to kill the other guy?" I then realized that effort and medical skill might have been able to repair Juan's heart, but it wasn't able to change his heart.

How do you change a heart? A few months ago I sat in a testimony meeting at the conclusion of a great youth conference. The spirit in the meeting was exceptionally strong. Lives and hearts had been changed at that conference. A young man got up to speak. He was obviously moved, but through his tears he said, "I have enjoyed being here and I have learned so much about the life I need to live, but I have done too many things in my life that I can't just brush off." Unable to continue, he sat down.

I immediately thought of Juan and a broken heart. I had just heard an Aaronic Priesthood holder who had made some mistakes in his life. He had felt the Spirit at the conference and knew the way he wanted to live, but was worried that his past mistakes would forever hold him back. Have you ever had similar feelings? You know those days when you feel you have made so many mistakes that there really is no point in trying to get back. The feelings are really quite common; most of us have experienced them at one time or another. When those feelings come, the important thing to remember is that there is a way back. There is a way to mend the broken heart.

The first step in mending a broken heart is to put one's mistakes in the proper perspective. Our earth life was designed to help us develop god-like qualities and characteristics. Developing Christian attributes requires experience, and with experience comes the inevitability of making mistakes. "Without both agency and some experience with opposition (experience that includes the mistakes that go with practice), it is not possible to have real learning—or real progress toward life, joy, and meaning" (Bruce C. Hafen, *The Broken Heart* [Salt Lake City: Deseret Book, 1989], p. 136).

During my high school years, on almost any Saturday during the winter you could find me snow skiing. I wasn't Olympic material by anyone's definition, but I loved the feeling of racing down the slopes with the wind and snow blowing into my face and the hope that this week I would miss the big trees! I'll never forget what my first ski instructor told me. He said, "You'll know you are learning when you begin to fall more often." That didn't make much sense to me then. I thought the whole purpose was to get down the mountain upright! However, as I skied more frequently and began to try more difficult techniques, I did fall more often—at least at first.

The lesson became clearer: mistakes are a natural part of our experience on earth. While we don't seek nor condone mistakes, actual growth comes as we learn from those mistakes and make resolute strides forward. Just as the skier never becomes truly skilled by skiing on the "beginner" slope year after year, we could hardly learn to become like our Heavenly Father if we were living in a world where we weren't allowed to make mistakes.

From the beginning, Father realized the importance of learning by experience. He knew that as we practiced using our free agency we would make mistakes, becoming unworthy to return to him. Therefore he provided a Savior for us before the world had even been created. "And he shall go forth, suffering pains and afflictions and temptations of every kind; and this that the word might be fulfilled which saith he will take upon him the pains and the sicknesses of his people" (Alma 7:11).

It is only natural for us to stumble and fall at times as we go through life. A major part of our lives will be spent in doing our best to put off the natural man and become as a child (see Mosiah 3:19). The problem arises not when we make mistakes but when we don't make the distinction between ourselves and our mistakes. The proper perspective, then, is to realize that we are children of a loving Heavenly Father, with the genuine potential of becoming like him, and that the process by which we become like him is one of experience that includes the possibility of making mistakes. Satan would have us lose that perspective and dwell on the mistake rather than on the potential for growth.

The second step to mending a broken heart is to avoid spiritual adventurism. One of Satan's greatest deceptions is that you can get as close to sin as possible but as long as you don't "go all the way" you'll be just fine. This is simply not true.

Several years ago, while teaching Spanish at the Missionary Training Center, I had a particular missionary who had a difficult time in learning the language. The frustration continued to grow daily, and it soon became obvious that something had to be done to defuse some of the tension. I thought that a friendly game of one-on-one basketball was just what this Elder needed, so on his next preparation day we met in the gym for the game. No one had warned me that my Elder had lettered in high school basketball for three years straight. I learned a valuable lesson that after-

noon: If you want to win, never, never go one-on-one with someone who is more experienced than you are. You will lose every
time.

Satan has almost six thousand years more experience at this
game called life than we do. He knows what works with teenagers
and has used those techniques on millions of young adults
through the years. He is well acquainted with the power of peer
pressure. Satan knows how to use situations and circumstances
to tempt and distract us. And as if that didn't give him enough ad-
vantage, all too often we get the adventurous spirit. There are
days when it seems we are confident that we can beat Satan at
his own game and by his own rules. When we work to mend a
heart that has been broken by sin, we can't play one-on-one with
Satan. We have to stay as far away from him as possible, because
as sure as we play with someone more experienced than we are,
we will lose.

A healing heart will hurt. Just as a patient recovering from
surgery will be sore for days or weeks, some spiritual soreness is
natural as the heart heals.

While I was a medical student in southern California I became
friends with Tom, a classmate who came from a strict, religious
family. He had been president of the Christian Medical Society in
college and also had been very active in his minister father's
parish at home. But Tom had found a new sense of freedom in
Los Angeles and had begun living quite a different life. One afternoon, while riding with him on a ski lift, I asked him if he felt
guilty about abandoning his strict standards. He looked at me
and in an almost apologetic tone said: "Curt, God doesn't want
me to feel guilty, he wants me to be happy; besides, Jesus will
save me from my sins."

God certainly wants us to be happy, but what my friend
didn't realize is that true happiness comes as we learn from our
mistakes and actively mend our hearts. What is more, the Savior
will save us *from* our sins but not *in* our sins. We are ultimately
responsible for our mistakes and for growing from them.

It was ironic that Tom kept insisting that when he got married,
graduated from medical school, and moved away from Los Angeles he would get back to his former standards. This brings to
mind a remark by Elder Marvin J. Ashton: "We often avoid taking
action because we tell ourselves that our problem was caused by
circumstances or people beyond our control. Therefore, we think

we can abdicate our responsibility, and we find ourselves hoping that other people or a change of conditions will solve our difficulties. Rather, it is our responsibility to repent—to change, and to move forward without delay." (*Ensign*, May 1983, p. 32.) Mending the heart can be painful, but should not be incapacitating. "For godly sorrow worketh repentance to salvation . . . but the sorrow of the world worketh death" (2 Corinthians 7:10).

As the heart begins to mend we need to remember that healing, both physical and spiritual, is a process and not an event, and though we feel better day by day, a wounded heart can't heal overnight. It will take time. President Spencer W. Kimball wrote: "Certainly self-mastery is a continuous program—a journey, not a single start. Men do not suddenly become righteous any more than a tiny acorn suddenly becomes an oak. Advancement to perfection can nevertheless be rapid if one resolutely strides toward the goal." (*The Miracle of Forgiveness* [Salt Lake City: Bookcraft, 1969], p. 210.) When you get discouraged with what may seem to be a lack of progress in mending your own heart just remember these few lines.

> Stick to your task till it sticks to you;
> Beginners are many, but enders are few.
> Honor, power, place, and praise
> Will always come to the one who stays.
>
> Stick to your task till it sticks to you;
> Bend at it, sweat at it, smile at it, too;
> For out of the bend, and the sweat, and the smile
> Will come life's victories after a while.
> (Quoted in Paul H. Dunn, *Seek the Happy Life*
> [Salt Lake City: Bookcraft, 1985], p. 47.)

A young man shared with me his personal struggle with pornography. As a fourteen-year-old he had glanced through a pornographic magazine at a convenience store near his home. He was a good Latter-day Saint, but he made some mistakes. A few glances quickly became a habit. He tried for months to break the habit, but the store was so centrally located that he passed by it almost every day. The temptation was too strong.

He finally came to the conclusion that the only way to truly overcome the problem and let his heart heal would be to never again use the road in front of that store. It took concentrated effort for several months as he went out of his way to avoid the store and thus the pornography. When he related the experience to me, I asked him how long it had been since he had driven in front of the store. His smile told me what I wanted to know, as proudly he said, "Three years, three long years!" Life's greatest victories require patience as well as effort.

All of us have done things in our lives that we "can't just brush off." Some of you may even feel as though your mistakes will forever hold you back. It is my prayer that you will understand that your broken heart can mend. You must have the proper perspective toward your mistakes, and you must take the responsibility to grow from them. It will take time, but because of the Savior's sacrifice for us, our mistakes will certainly become stepping-stones and not stumbling blocks as we actively strive to mend our broken hearts.

Curtis Galke is a captain in the U.S. Air Force, working as a family physician as well as a flight surgeon. He has served as a seminary teacher and as a Spanish instructor at the Missionary Training Center. His interests are music, water and snow skiing, and running. He and his wife, Alethea, are the parents of one son and live at Howard Air Force Base in Panama.

CHAPTER 19

The
Qualifying Trials

Kathryn S. Smith

It was one of those incredible autumn mornings. The leaves were gold and red, and the sun pierced through them like fingers of fire dripping diamond sparkles into the morning crispness. I walked a mile from my grandfather's ranch to the bus stop, and the ride into school from there was another half an hour. That morning's bustle on the bus was typical. All of us were chattering, and the engine noise forced us to yell in order to be heard. The ordinary stops took us patiently along our route into town, and it wasn't until almost the end that a young man stepped on.

I was fourteen. It is very important that you understand that, because I had never before felt the gripping emotion that swept my heart away. I was startled by the young man's presence. I felt immediately that I knew him, and in fact, I knew I loved him.

Now, you must realize that I did not commonly step into the realm of romance. In fact, when my daughters look at my high school photographs they ask me, "Mom, you didn't really go outside *looking* like that, did you?" I did. I had this stringy ponytail and black cat-eye glasses. I sat on the front row at school and took notes madly. I was sure that if I got A's it would reveal some marvelous trait about me, and so I was the eager student. I was also a freshman.

A sudden tunnel of light between "him and her" filled the bus. You've seen the old movies? The music swells; the lights dim, and they rush across the room to each other? He didn't rush. He didn't even *look* at me; I was having the movie by myself. But one thing *was* certain: I knew I recognized him, and I was completely confused.

Weeks passed, and one day when he stepped on the bus he paused by my seat and asked if he could sit down.

I tried not to faint. Weakly, I smiled. "Please do," I replied with whatever voice I could muster. He sat down and, to my surprise, talking with him was incredibly easy. The words flooded out like waves on a familiar seashore. We laughed; we listened. I watched him in disbelief. Where had this familiarity come from?

One day he looked at me intently and asked, "Kathy, have you ever heard of Joseph Smith?" I stopped. He was giving me a quiz. Let's see (I rummaged around in my memory)—there was George Washington, Abraham Lincoln . . . my mind was blank. I shook my head, embarrassed. I was the one who sat on the front row and took notes, and I had flunked the quiz.

"Well, we'll have to do something about that," he announced firmly. The next day he marched me into my homeroom teacher's classroom and told him I needed a copy of the Book of Mormon. The teacher opened a drawer and handed him a small black paperback with a golden statue embossed on one corner of the cover. My friend took it and opened it to Moroni chapter 10 verses 3-5.

"Read it, Kathy," he urged. He meant out loud, in front of everyone, right then. If there was anyone listening, I didn't notice. The words flowed out, and I felt a stirring of something I had known long before: "And when ye shall receive these things, I would exhort you that ye would ask God, the Eternal Father, in the name of Christ, if these things are not true; and if ye shall ask with a sincere heart, with real intent, having faith in Christ, he will manifest the truth of it unto you by the power of the Holy Ghost. And by the power of the Holy Ghost ye may know the truth of all things."

He bore his testimony. Right there in homeroom; right there in front of anyone who might choose to notice! He looked at me clearly and solemnly (and with those amazing eyes) and promised me that if I read the book and prayed about it I would know that it was true. I did not doubt him.

I was so entranced by the Book of Mormon that I read it as I walked in the halls at school between classes. If a teacher was slow in starting the lesson, I would sneak open its pages and read. I took it with me literally everywhere. I sat on it at the dinner table; if I went to the movies, it was in my purse. I found it magnetic, and the words inside were familiar and fascinating.

And so the journey began for me. How did your journey begin? Each of us must one day take the challenge and seek for himself to *know* that the Book of Mormon was revealed to Joseph Smith exactly as he said it was. If we do not know that for sure, we will never make it. The promise rests within the pages, quietly, patiently waiting for you and me to test it.

My friend took me to seminary every morning after that. His ride assured me it was "on the way." *How* ten miles out of town is on the way to *anywhere* never occurred to me, but someday in the spirit world I will find that kind, nameless driver and thank him. I listened; I read; I prayed. The witness came.

It was a peaceful autumn day once again. I was now fifteen, and I was studying in my living room, intensely working on a research paper for school the next day. No doubt the Book of Mormon was sitting on my desk, but I was not thinking about it. I suddenly felt a force grab me as if strong hands were grabbing my collar and throwing me back into my chair. A blast from a jet engine would not have been more jolting. I was filled with the words in my mind, "Kathy, the Book of Mormon is true."

Do you realize what that meant? It meant that Joseph Smith really did speak to our Father in Heaven in the grove of trees, as he said he did. It meant that truth was available to me if I would seek it—would choose it. The ball was in my court.

I had a family who did not appreciate my interest in what they have for years referred to as "that religion." My father, whose respect and love I had been trying to earn all my life, laughed at my earnest youthful representation of the spiritual witness I had received. "Kath," he began, "you don't need a crutch to lean on. Religion is like a drug that weak people use because they can't face up to life."

My best girlfriend, the one I trusted and valued the most next to my young LDS friend who had offered me the gospel, said to me, "Kathy, you want it to be true, so your emotions have fooled you into believing that you felt what you felt." I listened sadly to my favorite people tell me that what I had learned was not real. But I knew they were wrong. I knew what I had been told; I knew my Father in Heaven knew it, and it was at that moment that I realized that I had to choose between my testimony and my earthly parents and friends. I was baptized; I had found the right door out of the maze.

If you think, however, that choosing to follow the pattern set out so lovingly and clearly by our Father in Heaven will remove persecution and temptation and doubt, then you are very young in your gospel experience. The moment we choose God, Satan declares war, and the real artillery begins. It is at this moment that the "qualifying trials" commence their refining process. We are here to prove our loyalty, to prove our ability to commit ourselves, to prove our love. "Wherefore, the Lord God gave unto man that he should act for himself. Wherefore, man could not act for himself save it should be that he was enticed by the one [power] or the other." (2 Nephi 2:16.) If it was easy, what would we prove?

Satan, thinking to destroy us, helps us in our qualifying trials by calling into play every trick he holds in his bag. And remember, he has been gathering these tricks for a long time!

I believe that he attacks us in at least three categories:
—persecution within relationships
—personal temptations
—feelings of self-doubt

The night that he baptized me, my friend held me dripping wet in his arms and whispered in my ear, "Remember Kathy, the Church is perfect, but people are not." I did not understand the wisdom that he spoke from his youthful experience, but I have since learned exactly what he meant. In their struggling humanness, people hurt each other. As we stretch to become what we have learned is right, others are threatened by the changes in our attitudes and priorities.

One beautiful young convert eagerly took her discovery home to her parents last summer. Aged twenty-one, successful in each of a long string of beauty pageants she had entered, she found the gospel along her path. Happier than she had ever been, she opened her heart to her family. "It's a cult! You can't believe it! They brainwash their members!" Her mother and father were devastated and refused to listen. Alone and confused, she walked away from them.

Another young man, also twenty-one, took the news of his baptism home to his quiet, loving father, who smiled gently and told him that "he had never found organized religion to be very helpful." He expressed the family's sadness that the son had chosen to separate himself so completely from the traditions that the family had shared for so long. This young man sat at my table with tears streaming down his cheeks and cried, "I don't think I can do it any more."

When the ones we love the most disbelieve what we have felt, it shakes our innermost core. But Joseph Smith's words still echo the anchor we must cling to: "I had seen a vision; I knew it, and I knew that God knew it, and I could not deny it" (Joseph Smith—History 1:25). We have to turn within to the strength that lies undiscovered there. The Spirit will hold our hand while for a time we walk alone.

A second force that blares its horn is our attraction to the "treasures of the world." I used to say that the only ones who do not appreciate rich relatives are the ones who do not have them. My grandmother set up a trust fund for each of her grandchildren to attend a university anywhere in the world. I was fully expected to go back East to school, and when I decided to attend "the Y" my parents asked if I was talking about the YMCA. Watching the elegant circles of society melt away—the beautiful clothes, the rich ease that I had observed whenever I visited my father's family home or those of his friends—I felt a tug at my sleeve.

"Men will wine and dine you there," I had been told. The picture of luxurious youthful womanhood was painted for me, and I saw that I could choose it if I wanted to. The romance of the nineties that is carefully painted for you in every movie you attend, in every television show you watch, and in most of the lyrics that you listen to, is indulgent and is wrapped up as a delicious dessert. I assure you that it is only a mirage.

Once, years ago, I decided to try a bite of that luscious dish and made the decision to give in to one of the temptations that I found particularly hard to resist. It was a biggie. On the morning of my decision I was combing my hair and putting on makeup as I did every other morning. I was looking at myself in the mirror, when suddenly there was a face. Without intending to be overly dramatic, may I say that I recognized the face although I do not remember ever seeing it before. It had gentle eyes, dark hair, and a soft short beard. The eyes were neither condemning nor angry. They were not disappointed or shocked. The eyes were simply sad and full of love.

"Are you leaving me, Kathy?" the face in the mirror asked inside my mind. I looked away, for I knew that he knew. But the face followed my inner eyes and was still looking at me sadly.

"Where are you going?" he questioned. I lowered my eyes, for I knew the answer.

"Nowhere," I responded. There was nowhere else to go. The Church of Jesus Christ of Latter-day Saints is, in fact, the only truth. Its teachings are real, and the quiet, determined, day-to-day pursuit of those goals is the only path to happiness. I learned on that morning that temptation is simply a counterfeit mirage. The mirage melts away as we pursue it.

The final onslaught that Satan throws at us is the fear that, regardless of what we do, it will not mean much in the big picture. We try and try and no one notices. The poster caption reads, "When I do good, nobody remembers, and when I do bad, nobody forgets." What difference will it make *what* I do? Who cares?

Besides the obvious answers to that (which we can all supply when we are not depressed and angry ourselves), there is the reality that we may never know what good our influence will do. However, we can be sure that if we make a genuine, consistent effort it will count for our *own* good. T. S. Eliot wrote: "Ours is only in the trying. The rest is not our business."

Apparently Abinadi, the Book of Mormon prophet who was burned to death in the court of the wicked Nephite king, Noah, never knew in this life whether his prophecies or teachings had influenced anyone. He was sent into an apostate community to call them to repentance. It is not recorded whether Abinadi was ever aware that one set of listening ears would hear him, that one man, hearing his words, would repent. Was it worth the sacrifice of a prophet? For one man? That one man was Alma, who himself became one of the most influential prophets of the Book of Mormon. Every member of the Church, both in his own time and now in our time, has felt the touch and influence of Alma's words. Through him, we benefit from Abinadi's faithful willingness to do what he was guided to do. How do we know whom we might touch? who might be listening? who might be watching?

A young boy, prematurely given the throne of the ancient kingdom of Judah at age eight when his father the King died, reigned for thirty years. Before the days of King Josiah's influence the people had chosen to worship idols, to forget their Israelite traditions and teachings, and when he took the throne the people had completely deserted those teachings. King Josiah was righteous. His father was evil, his sons were evil, but he himself "did that which was right in the sight of the Lord, and . . . turned not aside to the right hand or to the left" (2 Kings 22:2).

Josiah sent the prophet Hilkiah to restore the temple, to take the funds available to him and repair it. The scriptures were found inside the temple and were read to King Josiah. He was horrified to see how far his people had strayed from the truth. He ordered that all the pagan temples and shrines be destroyed, had their practitioners put down, and challenged all his people to return to practicing the law of Moses appropriately. For the time of his reign, from 641 B.C. to 610 B.C., the kingdom of Judah enjoyed a reformation that greatly increased the general level of righteousness.

Then the young king died in battle in 610 B.C., and his son immediately returned to pagan practices and idol worship. The Lord was forgotten, and all the improvements of Josiah's reign were lost (see 2 Kings 23:30-37). What good had his righteousness done anyone? Why did the Lord drop this pearl of a young man into such a cesspool of evil? Why did he choose to send him on earth during such a vile time?

I struggled with that story when I first taught early-morning seminary. Then I thought about the dates. Ten years later, six hundred years before Christ's birth, the Book of Mormon *story* began. Lehi was a young father, a young man himself, during some of that thirty-year period of King Josiah's reign. While Lehi was growing up, while he was marrying and starting his family, more and more people were striving to follow Josiah's leadership in righteousness. Because of Josiah's commitment to the Lord, Lehi and Sariah were raised in a society that must have included many God-fearing people, good role models. Was there anything good that came from that moment in time? Was there any reason to place Josiah at the helm of Judah in the middle of that stormy century? The answer is obvious. Millions of souls have been and are being influenced by the book that came from Lehi's progeny.

My own young missionary friend only had one baptism to his credit. He introduced me to the gospel, and three short years later he died in Vietnam. He wanted to serve his country. I am so grateful for his willingness to stand up for what he believed; to stand there with a copy of the Book of Mormon in his hand, in a public school, in homeroom, and declare to me his surety that God answers honest prayers. Was his influence felt? Is my life worth that courage? If I have influenced anyone ever, the influence of my friend filters through. "Ours is only in the trying. The rest is not our business." The rest is Heavenly Father's business.

The trials that will come to us will be as uniquely personal and suited to our private individuality as will the blessings that will come to us as we remain faithful. We are here to qualify for the kingdom of God. We are here to pave the way for the second coming of the Savior, and he will use our example and our influence to strengthen others as we pass through the refiner's fire. The durability we will acquire through these refining experiences will carry us through any experience we may be expected to endure.

Kathryn S. Smith, a middle-school teacher (English and French) in Provo, Utah, has four children. Among her interests are writing, theater, and horseback riding. In 1966 she toured around the world in ninety days. In getting through her teen years Kathy was helped knowing she was "someone who mattered; I didn't give in to the magnets pulling me in different directions."

CHAPTER 20

Is Your Triangle Balanced?

Vivian R. Cline

Have you ever felt low? I mean *really* low. Nothing seems to be going right. There seems to be something wrong with everything and everybody. You just want to crawl under a shell somewhere and wish the world away!

When I have such feelings, something is wrong with my triangle. You see, a well-balanced person consists of three equal parts. There is a physical, an intellectual, and a spiritual side. Each side is equal in importance, and whenever we put too much attention on one particular side our triangle becomes off balance. The result is that we feel low or depressed.

For example, one day when I was feeling low I decided to have a nice long talk with myself. (Ever done that?) I looked at my triangle and went over each side individually. I felt okay about my physical side. I was getting plenty of rest and eating well. My intellectual side was fine too. I was reading the newspaper and a very interesting book. But when I got to my spiritual side I found that I was missing something. I was so busy eating, sleeping, and reading that I hadn't found the time to incorporate my daily scripture study. Also, my prayers were becoming pretty weak and not very regular.

I located my problem! Once identified, the situation was easily corrected. I read my scriptures every day and made a conscientious effort to pray with greater sincerity. Before I knew it I was feeling great again.

Though each of these three sides is equally important, society often places more attention on one particular side than the other two. That side is our physical side.

Why do we give so much attention to the physical side? Because that is the side everyone sees. Unfortunately people can't look at us and see how smart we are or what a close spiritual relationship we have with our Heavenly Father. All they can see is our exterior and whether we take care of it.

This physical side can be very deceiving. Have you ever judged someone by his or her physical appearance? We know the scriptures tell us, "Judge not, that ye be not judged," but we do sometimes form a quick opinion. Has that opinion ever been wrong? Have you ever been drawn to a person because of a beautiful exterior, only to find when you get to know that person there is absolutely nothing beautiful below the surface.

Some people may have perfect posture and a flawless appearance, but when they open their mouths you need a barf bag. Even though the physical side is perfect, the intellectual and spiritual sides of the triangle have been neglected. The triangle is off balance.

Along with being the most easily seen, the physical side is the only side that is limited. There is only so much that even the strongest and healthiest body can do. The limitations are especially clear in the matter of appearance. I know that good food and proper exercise can improve our looks somewhat as they increase our health and vigor. But generally speaking our genes have the last word, and we can't make dramatic improvements outside the pattern they establish. Despite many youthful longings, for example, "Which of you by taking thought can add one cubit unto his stature?" (Matthew 6:27.) So generally, once we feel good about the way we stand and walk, the way we wear our hair and makeup, and the way we dress, the only other thing we can do about our appearance is to maintain it. (And we can't even do that for all time—note the aging signs in older people.)

The mind and the spirit, however, are totally unlimited. We can become as intelligent and as spiritual as we desire. "The glory of God is intelligence" (D&C 93:36), and "whatever principle of intelligence we attain unto in this life will rise with us in the resurrection" (D&C 130:18).

Because the body is limited and the mind and the spirit are not, I like to think of my body as a car or vehicle which enables my mind and spirit to travel through this mortal existence. We all drive different models, makes, styles, and colors of vehicles. Some of us even drive semi-trucks! The point is that it doesn't matter what we drive as long as we have transportation. You can get in your sports car and I can get into a station wagon and we can both drive to our destination. We will both get there; the only difference is that I will get there for about twenty thousand dollars less than you!

My opinion, therefore, is that because our influence on our physical appearance is limited, the only reason why we should focus on it is to quickly master it so that we can move on to the things about us that are eternal: our minds and our spirits.

When I was a teenager I had a ball! I had a baseball, a basketball, and a tennis ball! Ball was number one in my life, second only, maybe, to boys. I played on all the school's athletic teams.

I quickly realized that in every family a basic level of academic achievement was required. In my home *A*'s were awesome, *B*'s were good, *C*'s were okay, but anything below that was unacceptable. I learned that if I had a mainstay of *B*'s sprinkled with a few *A*'s every now and then my parents would leave me alone, and I could play all the sports and date as much as I wanted.

While I was growing up in Georgia, my mother always told me: "There are three things in life you must do—graduate from high school, go to a university, and get married in the temple." She would drill it into my head over and over. "Remember, graduate from high school, go to a university, and get married in the temple." I heard it so many times that there was no question as to what I would do when I grew up. I would graduate from high school, go to a university, and get married in the temple.

One day at school a friend of mine approached me and asked if I planned on continuing my studies. I told her in no uncertain terms that not only was I going to a university but I wanted to go to BYU. She then asked if I had already been accepted. I said, "Not yet, but it's okay, because I'm a Mormon." My friend said: "I don't think so. You have to take entrance exams and apply like everyone else."

My friend was right. My religion did not alter my grades and test scores.

A few weeks after I mailed my application, a return letter came from BYU. Much to my shock and surprise, they had turned me down. I couldn't believe it. They had turned me down! I was devastated!

After much consoling from my parents, it was decided that I would go to a local junior college first and then try to get into the "Y" later.

Finally I was accepted at BYU. With great excitement I packed my bags and trunks, and off to Utah I went.

When I arrived I made a startling discovery. I found fifteen million gorgeous returned missionaries. Quickly I chose for myself a major and a minor. My major was Date-ology and my minor was Play-ology. I worked hard at both!

My grades were not fantastic that first year, but they were good enough. I played, dated, and had a blast!

In my second year at BYU I fell in love. Now, we all know that it is totally impossible to study when you're in love. Besides, I got engaged. How on earth can you be expected to study economics when you have more pressing decisions to be made. . . . like what your wedding colors are going to be. As a result, my grades weren't wonderful that year, either.

During my third year at BYU I was married and pregnant. I know you can't really appreciate or understand, but trust me when I tell you that it is impossible to study when you're throwing up into every available toilet. My first son, Talmadge, was born just ten days after my finals that semester.

As a result of all these good excuses for not studying, I left BYU under what is referred to as academic probation. That means, "Either you get your act together or you're out of here." That was okay though, because my mother's third goal for me, being married in the temple, had now been fulfilled.

I was happy. I had done everything my parents wanted me to do. I had graduated from high school, gone to a university, and got married in the temple.

But something was missing. You see, I had never really done very well in school and there seemed to be a little "tweety bird" that would sit on my shoulder and quietly tweet: "Vivian, do you have it and not use it? Or do you simply not have it?"

We hear lots of jokes these days about "airheads." Though it is wrong to categorize as less intelligent the women who take care of themselves physically, it is a common stereotype. Unfortunately, through the years I have frequently found this to be true. Many people in the beauty business focus on just their physical side and never progress to the mental and spiritual sides.

A few years ago that tweet of that bird got louder than I could stand. I decided to go back to school and find out the answer.

When I was a young woman, my first time at BYU was really tough. My parents would mail a check to me once a month and I would deposit it and write other checks. I didn't study. I just played real hard.

My second time at BYU was a little different. I was married and had five children. I taught finishing school classes for young women, was active in community affairs, and frequently traveled nationwide to speak.

I signed up with four major classes. The first class was Physical Science. For me, this was one of the most difficult basic general education classes the university required. I knew it would be tough.

The second class was New Testament. This was the last of my required religion classes.

The third was an Environmental Biology class. I knew I was up the creek without a paddle when I walked into the class and discovered that of the twenty-eight thousand students at BYU, only eighteen of them were in this class. Doom was confirmed when the professor stood up and announced that the class would be lecture only. There was no textbook.

Deciding that I didn't want to set myself up for complete failure, I signed up for a Child Psychology class. Surely I would do well in this class. After all, I had five specimens at home on whom to prove my ability.

During my first experience at BYU I would flit over to the Cougar Eat and have lunch. This second time I brought sandwiches from home and ate them between classes at the nearest study lounge.

About the only study time I could manage was between classes and on the bus I rode from my home in Draper to Provo and back.

After sixteen grueling weeks of this schedule my grades finally came in the mail. Now, I have done some pretty exciting things in life. Being on stage in the Mrs. Utah Pageant and wondering whether I was going to win was pretty exciting, but it doesn't hold a candle to how I felt as I opened the envelope containing my grades. You see, this was not a matter of whether the judges liked blondes or brunettes. It was the answer to that tweety bird as to whether or not I had "it."

With a deep breath I slowly opened the letter. When I saw my grades I couldn't believe my eyes.

Physical Science	A
Religion	A
Environmental Bio	B
Child Psychology	B+

Did I have it? Yes, I did. The problem is, I had never before used my intellectual side to its fullest potential. You can have all the potential in the world, but it is worthless unless you use it. So study hard, excel, and use the great potential that our Heavenly Father gave you. Intellectually be the best at whatever you choose.

The last part of our triangle is really the first part. It is the base of our triangle—the spiritual side.

Jesus said, "Seek ye first the kingdom of God" (Matthew 6:33). I have found in my own life that if I put my spiritual side first and seek the "kingdom of God" the other two sides seem always to fall into place. My Father in Heaven blesses me with more health and strength and intellectual ability.

In gaining a stronger spiritual side there are several vital steps. We must pray and read the scriptures daily, attend church and seminary, listen to uplifting music, keep our thoughts and actions clean, surround ourselves with stalwart and valiant friends, and find ways to serve our fellowman.

President Thomas S. Monson has said, "Prayer is the passport to spiritual power" (*Ensign*, November 1988, p. 70). We must pray both morning and night, both individually and with our family. Our Father in Heaven loves us just as our parents do, and he wants to hear from us regularly. Too often we say in our prayers what we think he wants to hear rather than what we really feel. We should talk to him as we do our best friends, for indeed he truly is our best friend and will never let us down.

Like many affiliated with the Church Educational System, I have the privilege of traveling to various parts of the country to speak at youth conferences. Several years ago I joined Brad Wilcox, Dottie Ralphs, and Craig Bradley. We were traveling to a conference in Nashville, Tennessee. Our itinerary took us from Salt Lake City to Dallas, Texas, where we changed planes, and then on to Nashville.

Now, I don't know whether you have had the experience of eating airplane food lately, but I truly believe that is the reason they have barf bags! It is so bad! So by the time we arrived in Dallas we were all starving to death.

We decided to get some hot dogs and drinks and eat them while we were waiting for our next plane. The only problem was that we each had carry-on bags with us. I made the recommendation that we go ahead and check in at the gate and see whether there was some place to put our bags.

As we approached the check-in counter I noticed a closet next to the ticket agent. I asked the agent if we could put our bags there while we went to get something to eat. She said that would be fine, that she would be there checking in passengers and the bags would be perfectly safe.

Brad proceeded to put everyone's bags into the closet; then off we went in search of food.

We were almost finished eating when we heard an announcement which said, "Flight 442 to Nashville, Tennessee, is now boarding at Gate 41."

No problem. We had already checked in, so we finished eating. Suddenly we heard an announcement which said, "Final boarding call for Flight 442 boarding at Gate 41."

Quickly we smashed the last bite of our hot dogs into our mouths as Brad reached into the closet and began retrieving our bags. He handed each of us our bags and then reached in to get his own, when suddenly his face turned white and his eyes got big.

"My bag is missing!" he exclaimed.

"No, it isn't, Brad," I retorted. "I saw you put it in there. You're just not looking closely." Hurriedly, I looked into the closet. Sure enough, the bag was gone.

Brad's eyes were still big as saucers when he said: "See this shirt and tie? I'm going to be in it for the next three days!"

"Didn't you have another bag that you sent through the baggage department with ours?" I asked.

"No," he replied. "Everything I had was in that carry-on bag. I'm going to be in these clothes . . . and underwear for the next three days!"

"No, you're not," I said excitedly. "We are going to find your clothes right now. Brad, you go this way. Dottie, you go that way. Craig, go this way. I'll go over there. Quick, before the plane leaves us."

Tearing off in different directions, we each went to frantically search for Brad's hanging suit bag (that, by the way, had a rip in it which was covered with duct tape).

Suddenly, something in my head said, "Vivian, pray!"

It sounded like a great idea to me. I would pray while I was searching for the bag . . . You know, faith and works!

"No," the voice said. "Pray the way you know you should pray."

I thought, "Like fold-my-arms prayer? Like bow-my-head prayer? Like right-in-the-middle-of-the-Dallas-International-Airport prayer?"

If you have ever felt the prompting of the Spirit you will know that it is usually soft, quiet, and often comes in threes. The minute I felt the prompting the third time, I stopped right in the middle of the airport, folded my arms, bowed my head and gave one of the shortest but most sincere prayers of my life. You see, I prayed with my heart and not my head.

"Dear Father in Heaven," I said, "we have a problem. My friend Brad has lost his luggage. If anyone has to lose their luggage, let it be me. I can find a way to replace my things, but my friend Brad can't. Please help us find it . . . and find it right now!" I then concluded my prayer.

Brad had just graduated from BYU and was teaching sixth grade. He and his wife had two little children. Beginning teachers don't make much money. Beyond the inconvenience at the youth conference, I knew it would be an extreme hardship for him to replace his things.

It was not twenty seconds after my prayer had closed that an announcement came over the P.A. system: "Will Brad Wilcox please report to gate 42?"

It was the next gate over. I ran as fast as I could.

"I'm Brad Wilcox's friend," I said. "Do you have his bag?"

There, lying over the check-in counter, was Brad's bag.

"Where did this come from," I asked with great surprise.

With reluctance the attendant said, "I'm not really sure, but probably someone picked it up by accident and was too embarrassed to return it."

I know where that bag came from, and I think you do too. However, the story doesn't end there.

With bag in hand I found Brad, and off we went to Nashville, just barely making our flight.

On the plane I told a very relieved and happy Brad what had

happened in finding the bag. That was a mistake. Brad, being the not-so-quiet person he is, told everyone at our youth conference about the experience. I was the talk of the conference. "Don't worry about anything," the young people would say. "We have Sister Cline with us. If you lose something, she will pray it back for you!"

The conference was wonderful. We could feel the Spirit in its fulness. Afterwards, however, a series of strange events began.

First, I flew back a day early. I never do that. But I had a severe back problem, and my physician requested that I get back as soon as possible.

Second, transportation was always provided me when I was traveling with a group. Not this time. My husband took me to the airport and picked me up.

Third, whenever my husband picks me up, he almost always brings the children so that they can see the planes. This time he didn't.

Last of all, we have two cars, a nice one and a little economy station wagon. When it's just the two of us we always take the nice car, and when we have the children we use the gummy station wagon so we don't have to worry about them messing it up. This time he drove the station wagon without the children.

As we waited for my luggage to come out of the carousel, I told my husband how badly I needed a new suitcase. Mine had seen years of use. The handle was half off, the seams were ripped, and the sides bore the scars of my many trips.

Just as the luggage came out, a beautiful piece of Samsonite arrived along beside it. The piece was beautiful. It had a hard, smooth finish and was adorned with handle and wheels. I mentioned to Doug that my luggage was shot and that I really needed a nice piece of luggage with wheels to take the pressure off my back. Doug agreed, and said that those bags were really expensive but someday we would get one.

We walked up to the car and Doug set my suitcase down. He opened the back door of the station wagon and carefully laid my carry-on bag across the back seat. Closing the door, he picked up my suitcase and put it on the luggage rack on top of the car. I thought how strange to put it on the luggage rack when the entire back end of the station wagon was empty. I almost opened my mouth to tell him that he should move it, but I thought, Vivian, that is what luggage racks are for. I didn't say a thing—I just got into the car.

On the way home I told Doug about everything that had happened at the Dallas Airport and the youth conference. He chuckled and said he thought it was great.

We pulled into the driveway of our home and Doug, being the perfect gentlemen he is, got out to open my car door. As he opened the door, he looked down at me and in his cool, calm, collective banker's voice said, "Your luggage is missing."

I laughed and told him that, after the experience I had just shared, I didn't think his joke was very funny. He didn't smile. I quickly exited the car to find it was no joke. My luggage *was* missing!

Visions of cars on I-15 running over my clothes, heat rollers, and other things passed through my mind. I panicked. Doug said, "Get back into the car. We'll trace our path from the airport back home and find it."

We traced every mile from the airport to our home. Guess what! No luggage.

When we pulled into our home driveway I began to cry. My husband said, "Honey, what's wrong?"

I retorted "Tomorrow you're going to be crying."

"Why?" Doug asked.

"Because all my makeup was in that bag!" I sobbed.

Not only my makeup but many other precious items were in that lost suitcase. My garments, my scriptures, a camera, and two 14-karat gold chain necklaces which my parents had given me for my thirtieth birthday. I was devastated.

Calmly Doug said: "Don't cry, honey. We have insurance. All you have to do is write down each item in the suitcase and what it will cost to replace it. The insurance company will send you a check and you can go shopping and replace everything with new. Think about it, Viv."

Suddenly the words to a special prayer blazed through my mind . . . "If anyone has to lose their luggage, let it be me."

"Oh, no!" I said. "Do you remember, Doug, what I told you happened at the Dallas Airport?"

When I repeated the words of my prayer to Doug, he exclaimed, "Vivian, don't you know the Lord hears and answers prayers?"

"Yes," I answered, "but I have never had one answered so quickly and literally!" While Brad's luggage had been found almost immediately, mine had literally become its replacement, as I had prayed it would. And now the Lord had blessed me with the ability to replace all my things with new!

My dear young friends, I stand as a witness that God does live and that he does hear and answer our prayers. That was the only prayer that I have had answered in twenty seconds. Sometimes it had taken twenty minutes, sometimes two months, and sometimes two years to receive an answer to my prayers. Not because Heavenly Father didn't have the answer, but because I am not always ready to receive his answer.

I earnestly pray that you will seek first the kingdom of God, using your triangle's spiritual base. Keep your triangle in balance always. God lives. He loves us. He cares about every detail and aspect of our lives.

Vivian R. Cline, an owner of a finishing school in Salt Lake City and director of the "Polish with Pleasure" workshop at BYU, was Mrs. Utah-America in 1980. She likes traveling, working with youth, playing softball, and reading the scriptures. She appreciates the "receptiveness and honesty" of young people. Vivian and her husband, Douglas, have five children.